P9-DUC-966

Walsh, John

Night on fire

DATE DUE

MAR 14 78			
DEC 3 80			
FEB 16 '88			
FEB 12 '92			
MAR 4 '02			
MAR 4 '0			
FEB 11			

Night on Fire

The battle about as it appeared to the thousands of spectators crowded along the English shore and atop Flamborough Head. (Oil painting by James Hamilton, 1854, "Capture of the Serapis by John Paul Jones," Yale University Art Gallery, gift of Mrs. Francis P. Garvan for the Mabel Brady Garvan Collection

Night on Fire

The first complete account of
John Paul Jones's greatest battle

by

John Evangelist Walsh

McGraw-Hill Book Company

New York / St. Louis / San Francisco / Düsseldorf
London / Mexico / Sydney / Toronto

Book design by Beverly G. Haw, A Good Thing, Inc.

1 2 3 4 5 6 7 8 9 0   M U B P   7 8 3 2 1 0 9 8

Library of Congress Cataloging in Publication Data

Walsh, John Evangelist, date
Night on fire.
Bibliography: p.
Includes index.
1.   United States—History—Revolution 1775–1783—
Naval operations.   2.   Bon Homme Richard (Ship).
3.   Serapis (Ship).   4.   Jones, John Paul, 1747–1792.
I.   Title.
E271.W2   973.3′5   77-26762
ISBN 0-07-067952-5

Dedicated
to the memory of

Lt. Wallace R. Franklin, USN
VF 11 Fighter Squadron
1950–1976

Aboard the *Bonhomme Richard*
he would have been at home

Other books by
John Evangelist Walsh

The Shroud
The Story of the Holy Shroud of Turin

Strange Harp, Strange Symphony
The Life of Francis Thompson

The Letters of Francis Thompson

Poe the Detective
The Curious Circumstances behind
the Mystery of Marie Roget

The Hidden Life of Emily Dickinson

One Day at Kitty Hawk
The Untold Story of the Wright Brothers

The Affair of Poe and Mrs. Osgood

Contents

Prologue

Samuel Eliot Morison, by far the most complete and capable of John Paul Jones's biographers, has called the battle between Jones's ship, the *Bonhomme Richard,* and the English frigate, *Serapis,* during the Revolutionary War, "a naval combat the like of which has never been fought before or since." That is undoubtedly true. While there have been single-combat engagements in which the cannonading at a distance was fiercer and of longer duration, the maneuvering of more classic design, and in which the fighting close-to played a larger part, there have been none in which all these elements came so explosively together. Assuredly, there has been no other in which the victorious captain stood finally in possession of the enemy's quarterdeck, while watching his own devastated ship go down.

Despite all this, however, and even though an unusual number of able writers have been drawn to the life and career of John Paul Jones, the battle itself has never received the detailed attention that might have been expected. Morison himself, more concerned with Jones's whole life, accords it only a rather brief, almost matter-of-fact treatment, saying at one point that the fighting was "difficult to imagine, impossible to describe in detail." In this view, it appears, all of Jones's biographers have concurred, none making an effort to go much beyond the story as it has been recounted over and over, with slight changes in approach and emphasis, for two centuries. In fact, while some portions of the action have become familiar through repetition, other portions, among the most important, even now remain question marks. Why did Jones, for example, not send a boarding party against the English ship for more than two hours, even though that was his whole purpose in grappling? Herein, I trust, that long-unanswered question—along with a number of others—is finally cleared up.

This failure to focus more narrowly on the details of the battle has been unfortunate, for it leaves unfinished the story of what was perhaps the most spectacular career in American naval history. Further, and more to the point, without this epic encounter Jones would not today be enshrined as he is in the pantheon of America's greatest heroes. While he did perform one or two other deeds that would at least have kept his memory green, it was his remarkable triumph over the British frigate that made him a legend, and earned him honored burial within the precincts of Annapolis. "He gave our Navy," reads the inscription on the splendid tomb, "its earliest traditions of heroism and victory."

It is true that a great deal of what took place in that flaming chaos off the British coast cannot now be recovered. Yet it is still quite possible (*pace,* Morison) to reconstruct the battle's progress in some detail, to chart its ebb and flow, to show many of its principals in action, even to suggest some small idea of its awful magnificence. Such an effort, however, if it is to be faithful to the reality, must depend entirely in the first instance on primary documents, avoiding the often imaginative, frequently inaccurate descriptions of many later writers. The full truth, in all its many subtle facets, regarding an incident that occurred in such physical isolation, can only be derived from evidence preserved by eyewitnesses. Luckily, few such battles of the days of sail have been so well documented by participants as this one.

John Paul Jones himself, in his several reports, left various descriptions of the action, and Captain Pearson of the *Serapis* one, his long report to the British Admiralty. Jones's first officer, Richard Dale, not only prepared a brief account of his own (for inclusion in the first biography of his commander), but provided the information that largely underlies two secondary accounts. One of the *Richard*'s other officers, Midshipman Nathaniel Fanning, and one of its gunners, John Kilby, each left in their general reminiscences a circumstantial report of what had taken place. In addition, there are a number of other documents, such as log entries, affidavits concerning a particular phase of the action, and the transcript of Captain Pearson's court-martial (an automatic procedure for captains who lost their ships).

None of the eyewitness accounts are complete or consecutive narratives of the battle, nor were they intended as such. Each man wrote what he understood to be the truth, inserting such details as he could recall, or that seemed significant. Each viewed the action from his own position and background, and through the haze not only of time but of personal prejudice. Yet there is little outright contradiction, at least little that is insoluble, and there is much basic agreement.

In the task of interpreting these documents, five secondary accounts have proved valuable in the handling of obscure points. Three of these are full biographies of Jones, those by Captain Alexander Mackenzie (1841), Lincoln Lorenz (1943), and Morison (1959). The other two authors, while writing biography, confined themselves largely to Jones's career in the Revolution: James Fenimore Cooper (1825 and 1842), and Admiral (then Captain) Alfred Thayer Mahan (1898). While the present account does not always agree with what these men have had to say, it would have been the poorer without the stimulus they provided. Other works that have yielded special insights are listed separately in the Bibliography.

In reconstructing this unparalleled battle, I have resisted the sometimes strong temptation to stray into the general history of naval combat in the Revolution, natural background to the story of John Paul Jones. Nor have I gone deeply into the events of Jones's previous or later life. Instead I have kept my focus rigidly on the battle itself, on the events of the morning leading up to it, and on the happenings of the following day. My single purpose, my one constant aim, has been to answer to the fullest extent possible the central question: What, exactly, took place on those tumultuous, smoke-shrouded decks where over five hundred brave men fought for an interminable three and a half hours, breathing death in the very air?

Night on Fire

Behold, I am making my words
in your mouth a fire, and this
people wood, and the fire shall
devour them.

Jeremiah 5:14

1

Rendezvous at Flamborough Head

Standing on the scrubbed quarterdeck of His Majesty's frigate *Serapis,* Captain Richard Pearson trained his telescope on the low Yorkshire coast, some two miles to starboard. He was searching for any warning signals that might have been set up ashore. If enemy activity or sightings had been reported in these waters, red flags would be flying.

Towering above Pearson's head there rose an immense cloud of sail, each of the ship's three masts carrying a full press of canvas. The wind, very light and blowing from the southwest, was directly against the *Serapis* and the ship was now on the port tack, heading inshore. Riding on the calm waters between the sleek frigate and the hazy coast, a multitude of merchant vessels spread to north and south, their bellied sails gleaming in the bright morning sun.

Eight days before, Pearson had departed Christiansund, Denmark, as escort for a convoy of seventy ships, laden mostly with stores for the Royal Navy. It had been an anxious eight days, for he had only one other warship to support him, a lightly armed sloop, the *Countess of Scarborough*. But the passage across the North Sea had been uneventful. Especially, there had been no sign of the Yankee privateersmen who, since the start of the Revolution, had plagued English waters.

Some five hours before, at daybreak on 23 September, 1779, he had made his landfall at Whitby. Here, part of the convoy had broken off and turned north for Scotland, leaving Pearson with forty-one vessels still in his care to continue south for London. Though he had herded his charges as close inshore as he could, posting the two escorts on the outside about a mile apart, the sprawling merchantmen remained an enticing target for a daring raider. And, depending on the winds, London was still three days away.

By 11 A.M. the foremost ships of the strung-out convoy were starting to come up on jutting Flamborough Head, a lofty chalk promontory that interrupted a sixty-mile sweep of the British coast from Robin Hood's Bay to the Spurn. It was about this time that Pearson's telescope picked up the mottled gray ramparts of ancient Scarborough Castle, just north of the Head, and he quickly spotted the large red flag waving from a staff. In the waters below the Castle a small cutter, also flying a red flag, was just setting out, evidently to intercept the *Serapis*. Within a half hour, after threading its way through the convoy, the cutter was alongside.

On deck, a messenger presented a letter from the bailiff of Scarborough. Reading it, Pearson saw in dismay that his arrival home could not have been more badly timed, and that the last leg of his journey was not to be free of concern. The American raider, John Paul Jones, the letter said, was cruising the English coast with a flying squadron of at least four ships, three of them large, and was causing great commotion and fear among the shipping and in the seacoast towns.

One week ago, the messenger explained, Jones had actually sailed into the Firth of Forth and had threatened, unless a huge ransom was paid, to lay in ashes the defenseless town of Leith. Only the providential arrival of a strong gale had saved the despairing townspeople, blowing Jones's ships out of the Firth. He had also made threatening gestures at Newcastle, but had sailed away. Then, just the evening before, not twenty-four hours ago, Jones's marauders had been observed some miles at sea standing south for Flamborough Head. Unless he had crossed the channel back to France, he was probably still hovering along the coast to the south in search of prey—if he had not already landed somewhere to sack a town or lay it under ransom.

To make matters worse, no ships of the Royal Navy were anywhere in sight, though after the Leith incident urgent calls for assistance had been dispatched by messenger to the Admiralty in London. In all the towns along the coast, from Whitby to Hull, defenses had been shored up and the local militias called out to oppose a landing. Coasting vessels by the hundred had put hastily into the nearest ports, straining facilities to the point where most could not be berthed but only crowded together and chained.

Captain Pearson didn't have to inquire who this John Paul Jones was. Since the year before nearly all of England was familiar with the name. During one sensational three-day period in April 1778, Jones had engaged in a series of actions round the north of England that had sent a wave of shock through the populace, still all too vividly remembered.

First, at the port of Whitehaven, he had personally led a large raiding party ashore at dawn. Holding the townspeople at bay, the raiders had spiked cannon and set fire to shipping, escaping back to their own vessel without a casualty. It had been a very small and brief invasion, but it had been the first time in memory that an enemy had landed with hostile intent on an English shore. It had brought home to the ordinary British citizen, as nothing else had done, the reality of the Revolution then raging in the far-off American colonies.

The day after that, only twenty miles from Whitehaven, Jones had calmly landed another party at St. Mary's Isle in order to kidnap the Earl of Selkirk and hold him hostage for the release of American naval prisoners in English jails. The Earl had been absent from home, so Jones's party had confiscated the treasure of the house, 160 pounds of silver plate. Then, incredibly, on the very next day, while ships of the Royal Navy were rushing to intercept him, Jones enticed into battle in the Irish Sea His Majesty's sloop of war, *Drake*. Jones's vessel at that time, the *Ranger*, was also a sloop of war, carrying an armament of eighteen 9-pounder cannon, about equal to the twenty 6-pounders of the *Drake*. After an hour's murderous broadsiding, the Englishman had struck his colors and Jones had sailed serenely away, his hold full of prisoners, and with the battered sloop as prize.

Since then, around the figure of John Paul Jones in England, in gossip, news accounts and even in street ballads, rumor had shaped a legend of the man, not as an intrepid naval officer but as a hated pirate. Lurid stories were told about his cruelties toward his foes, his ruthlessness toward his own men, his dark and evil visage, his cutthroat heart, his corsair's fighting costume, which included a rakish bandana on the head or a Scotch bonnet, and a personal armament of a dozen pistols jammed into a wide sash at his waist. Now it appeared that the pirate was back again, raising an uproar along a coast that had once been thought unassailable, by his mere presence in English waters hurling defiance at half the British navy.

On finishing the bailiff's letter, Pearson did not hesitate. Though identification had not been positive, in all likelihood the ships sighted the day before were indeed those of Jones. At that very moment he might be lurking only a few miles away, hidden under the southern flank of Flamborough Head. If Jones's rapacious eye should fall on this large convoy, protected by only a frigate and a sloop, there could be no doubt of the action he would take. He might first throw his whole squadron against the escorts, or perhaps would send part of it direct for the convoy. Either way, it seemed that a dozen or more merchantmen were in imminent peril of being captured or sunk. The bailiff's letter had estimated the armament of the larger ships to be forty or fifty guns each, but it hardly mattered. A pitched battle against three large ships of war, even if their armament separately was inferior to his own, could promise only certain defeat for the *Serapis*. Yet that was the fate, Pearson saw unflinchingly, that he must court if Jones should appear on the scene. He must provide time for the convoy to run for cover.

It was now past noontime and the forward ships of the convoy were almost abreast of Flamborough Head. Pearson gave swift orders: Hoist signal flags calling all ships to bear down under the lee of *Serapis*—to get north of their escort—and fire off two guns to reinforce the command. By this time a half dozen more of the merchantmen were already far south, stretching for the Head, and that meant they would have to wear round and run back before the wind. As the sound of the cannon boomed over the water—once, twice—Pearson held his own course southward, awaiting the return of the leaders.

Suddenly, from the two or three lead ships, those that had begun the long pull round the Head, there came the repeated firing of guns. Peering through his telescope, Pearson saw that these vessels had let fly their topgallant sheets and were frantically tacking in an effort to turn back north—all except one, the foremost. This lone ship appeared to be pressing on round the Head, perhaps intending to make a run for nearby Bridlington Bay.

The alarm, Pearson knew, could mean only one thing, that strangers had been sighted. If the unidentified ships were indeed those of Jones, then he must hurry to place the *Serapis* squarely between the American and the scurrying convoy. To increase speed he ordered out all studding sails—hanging at the outer ends of the yardarms on both sides, they made the ship appear almost as if it had wings—then instructed his lieutenant to announce "Clear ship for action!"

For his fateful rendezvous, Pearson could at least be grateful that he had under him a formidable fighting ship, one of the newest, most powerful and best-equipped frigates in His Majesty's service. Barely six months off the stocks, the *Serapis* was among the first of Britain's warships to be fitted with a copper bottom (the thin plates, nailed on, inhibited marine growth and increased a ship's speed by as much as a knot). Heavily armed for her size, she carried a total of fifty guns, throwing a 300-pound broadside.

On the upper gun deck (just below the open main deck) were twenty 9-pounders. Below this, another deck held the main battery, twenty long-barreled 18-pounders. The *Serapis* was thus a two-decker, carrying two full batteries, each of which was protected by having a deck overhead. Lacking the now old-fashioned poop deck, her sleek hull, measuring 140 feet in length and 38 feet in the beam, had been constructed along new lines, increasing her maneuverability. Her sides were painted black, with a broad band of yellow running along each of the two rows of gunports. From her stern flagstaff flew the huge ensign of the Royal Navy's Red Squadron: a plain, blood-red field, with the Union Jack occupying the top inside corner.

In the character of her commander, the *Serapis* had been well served. Tall and well-built, with a face whose serious eyes and strong lines seemed molded to command, Captain Pearson could call on almost thirty years of Royal Navy experience, beginning as a midshipman in the Mediterranean Squadron. While his career had been steady rather than spectacular, he had served with distinction aboard a dozen different warships, and his coolness and skill in ship handling, especially, had earned the respect of all his superiors. Once, as a young first lieutenant on the seventy-four-gun flagship *Norfolk,* he was in temporary command, the captain having been disabled by an accident, when an awesome hurricane struck the area in which his squadron was cruising. While some of his consorts foundered, the twenty-nine-year-old Pearson brought the *Norfolk* through the violent, six-hour storm with such calm ability that his admiral promised him a captaincy. Only the untimely death of the admiral, and his youth, had prevented him from becoming one of the youngest captains at that time in the Royal Navy.

Though his experience of battle command was limited, on four occasions in the East Indies, three of them in fleet actions, Pearson had seen combat. He had been wounded once, at the siege of Pondicherry, and though in great distress had shown himself a man of mental as well as physical strength. Hit in the side by grapeshot, with two ribs broken, suffering internal bleeding, he had remained at his post for an hour, until the close of the action. He had now held his captain's commission for nine years and had already commanded two other frigates. For a brief time he had even operated in American waters, against Yankee privateers. Recalled to England early in 1779, he was given the newly built *Serapis,* then in the process of fitting out as a convoy escort.

Well pleased with his new assignment, Pearson had set eagerly to work. Forming as efficient a crew as possible—he immediately requested, and was given, more men—he proceeded in shaking down the tight, new vessel. His preparations had been interrupted for several weeks in the spring when an old complaint, rheumatism, flared up and he was furloughed home for a rest. But the delay had not been wholly unwelcome, for it gave him the infrequent pleasure of a leisurely visit with his wife, two daughters and four sons at the family home in Appleby, Westmoreland.

In its other officers, and particularly in its crew, the *Serapis* had been equally fortunate. Lieutenant John Wright, second in command to Pearson, possessed about twenty years of experience, more than half of them as a lieutenant. The second and third lieutenants, Michael Stanhope and Richard Shuckburgh, though young, were officers of promise. The highly trained, well-disciplined crew of nearly three hundred (including a detachment of Royal Marines), conscious of their navy's long tradition of valor, saw themselves as invincible in any fight on equal terms, standing a fair chance even against heavy odds. One good British tar, ran the confident boast, was worth three Yankee sailors any day.

Twenty miles south-southwest of Flamborough Head, close in to the wide-curving strand of Holderness, rode the American armed vessel *Bonhomme Richard*, under full sail. Standing on its high poop deck were several officers, each attired in a blue uniform coat, white knee britches and black tricorn hat. The eyes of all were turned south, beyond the *Richard*'s bow, fixed on a small brigantine that was straining against the wind a mile or so away. Trailing behind the *Richard* were the other ships of the squadron: frigate *Alliance,* frigate *Pallas,* and the *Vengeance,* a small corvette.

For more than two hours, since about eleven that morning, the *Richard* had been chasing the brig, anticipating an easy capture. But the little vessel had repeatedly managed to skip away, frantic to reach safety at the entrance to the Humber. The distance between the two was now rapidly closing, however. Soon a gun would speak from the *Richard*'s side, a shot would splash across the brig's bow, and the game would end with the brig docilely hove-to, taking aboard a prize party.

In command on the *Richard*'s quarterdeck at the moment was the ship's captain, John Paul Jones. Slightly smaller in stature than the other officers, he was neatly dressed in the same blue-and-white uniform, with extra gold on the buttonholes and piping, and two shoulder epaulets, indicating his rank as commodore of the squadron. At the age of thirty-two, and despite his lack of height, Jones was an impressive figure, with a slim, athletic build and a straight-backed carriage that hinted at unusual stores of energy. Under the tricorn hat the deeply tanned, clean-shaven face was lean of flesh, and the long chestnut hair was gathered at the back into a queue, sailor fashion. The dark hazel eyes were steady and direct in their gaze, yet behind their apparent calm, as more than one acquaintance had observed, there lurked a peculiar glint of wildness.

As the little brig tacked sharply in a last gallant effort at escape, from high in the *Richard*'s mainmast a loud call came suddenly from the lookout: Sail astern! Large ship, standing south round the Head, bearing north-northwest.

Reacting promptly, Jones gave a series of orders to his lieutenants: Arm the small pilot boat (decoyed into capture the day before) and send it with a detachment to take the brig, Lt. Lunt to command—bring the *Richard* about smartly and stand north toward the large ship—consorts to follow *Richard*. Within minutes, swivel cannon and muskets had been passed into the pilot boat, followed by Lt. Lunt and fifteen marines. Then the two vessels parted, the smaller setting a hasty tack southward, the other wearing slowly round and making north toward the lone sail.

While Jones had acted swiftly at the appearance of larger prey, he felt no particular relish at the prospect of making yet another capture. On this cruise he had already taken numerous prizes, many with valuable cargoes. But as he was only too well aware, he had not been given his command to seek out single ships, like any common privateer or letter-of-marque. Some six weeks before he had set sail from France with an open commission to repeat, and if possible surpass, the sensational deeds of his last year's cruise. He was to pick his own objectives, his own times, move as he deemed best in order to inflict maximum loss and embarrassment on the enemy. Yet in over a month of prowling round the

British Isles he had accomplished little, certainly had done nothing to justify the force at his disposal. And very shortly, in a week at most, he would have to return with his squadron to his home base in France.

Keenly disappointed, on this bright morning the disgruntled Captain Jones saw himself as very much a failure, especially when he recalled his confident predictions at the start. Departing from France he had solemnly promised, as he expressed it, "to go in harm's way," had vowed to return with laurels, "if I survive," and there had been few who doubted that he would again blazon his name in terror along the British coasts.

A man of supreme self-confidence, Captain Jones impressed all who knew him as eminently well fitted for a mission that required, in addition to masterly seamanship and tactical daring, an utter contempt for danger. Neither cold-blooded nor foolhardy, Jones welcomed danger, and thrived in its midst, because it was only out of such ultimate hazard that "glory" was born—and he never made a secret of his unbounded thirst for that most elusive of distinctions. It was the dream that gave substance, meaning, purpose to his life, a dream in which wealth and comfort played no part. "I have never served but for honor," he once proudly insisted, "I have never sought but glory."

In that attitude he was not essentially different from many other officers of the time, on either side, by land or sea. The quest for personal honor was only another way of expressing a more exuberantly patriotic approach to war, and in that sense "glory" was a word that sprang easily to the lips. But in the rare intensity of his desire, in his inflexibility of purpose, Captain Jones held a place apart.

Impetuous by nature, fretful of control, sharply aware of his superior abilities, his mind continually swarming with plans for action and for the improvement of the navy, he seldom hesitated to act or to speak out, especially on his own behalf. "Eccentricities and irregularities are to be expected of him," remarked John Adams in mild disapproval. "They are in his character, they are visible in his eyes." So volatile a presence does not always pass unresented, and Jones frequently encountered dislike and opposition. He lived, after all, in a very formal custom-burdened age, and it is hardly surprising that by many he was condemned as arrogant, self-seeking, crudely boastful. But there were many others, more conscious of his abilities than his manner, who wholeheartedly accepted him as America's most promising naval commander. "I consider this officer," said Thomas Jefferson, "as the principal hope of our future efforts on the ocean."

Jones's fierce drive to excel, usually, was unleashed only in official circles or when he strode a quarterdeck. In his casual behavior ashore it was not often obtrusive. Among friends he displayed a dry wit and spoke in a low, soft voice, his deportment gentlemanly almost to an extreme, as if he were deliberately reigning in the passion that smoldered underneath. Though he would vigorously press his superiors for full recognition of his merits, he was no mere indiscriminate braggart. "It was impossible to get him to talk about his great deeds," recalled one Paris friend, "but on all other subjects he willingly talked with a great amount of sense."

Though he sometimes wistfully dreamed of settling down with a wife to an existence, as he described it, "of calm contemplation and poetic ease," he was still unmarried, having indulged in a half dozen transient love affairs on both sides of the ocean. What appears to be the blunt truth about Jones and women was long ago put succinctly by his earliest biographer: "The only mistress to whom Paul Jones was ever devoted with all the powers of his heart and mind was *glory*, in pursuit of which he made no scruple at any time to set his foot on the neck of the gentle Cupid."

Unusual ambition had been a part of Jones's character from his youth. Born in Scotland in 1747, he was the son of John Paul, a gardener (the Jones was to come later). When only twelve years old he went to sea as an apprentice in the West Indies trade, and at seventeen he became third mate on a slaver. This was a traffic that disgusted him but in which he remained, for two years, simply because of the chance it offered a young man impatient to rise. At twenty-one he was master of a merchantman, a sixty-ton brig, and three years later he became both captain and part owner of a large, three-masted square-rigger.

During his decade at sea he had frequently called into American ports, especially in Virginia, where he was able to visit an older brother who had settled at Fredericksburg. Fascinated by the bustling freshness of the colonies, Jones had soon decided to follow his brother's lead, and in 1773 he made the move—though under circumstances that are still not well understood. This much is known: In the West Indies, at the port of Tobago, where Jones had just arrived with a cargo from England, a violent disturbance arose among his crew. In quelling the riot he ran his sword through the ringleader, killing him. To avoid an inquiry, perhaps also to avoid vengeance from the dead man's friends, he fled Tobago incognito and soon afterward turned up in Virginia with the name of Jones, acquired no one knows how or where, added to the John Paul.

At the start of the Revolution he was among the first to offer himself for the Continental navy, then a tiny, struggling service employing a few old ships, laughably insignificant when compared with England's ocean-dominating 500-ship fleet. Though his knowledge of naval matters was small, Jones threw himself into the task of learning, often studying far into the night, and his promotion was rapid. As a lieutenant on the ship *Alfred* he took part in a foraging expedition to the Bahamas, and it was in the same vessel that he had his first taste of ship-to-ship combat. Directing the fire of twenty 9-pounders on the lower deck, he learned more in a fifteen-minute exchange of broadsides with H.M.S. *Glasgow* than he had in all his previous hours of solitary study.

That encounter was indecisive. Shortly afterward, however, as acting captain of the sloop of war *Providence,* his unique talents were finally given some chance for display. During a six weeks' cruise, in addition to destroying part of the English fishing fleet in Canada, he captured no less than sixteen prizes and gave abundant proofs of his genius at ship handling. Once he cleverly rescued another American warship from the clutches of a large English frigate, then whisked the *Providence* herself to safety almost under the enemy's bow, leaving the frigate's captain shaking his head.

It was in November 1777 that he was dispatched to France as captain of the *Ranger,* assigned to carry the war to the enemy's homeland. On arriving in Quiberon Bay he found himself the recipient of an unusual honor, receiving the booming salutes of the French navy, the first time the Stars and Stripes had been officially hailed in Europe. Five months later came his descents on Whitehaven and St. Mary's Isle, and his capture of the *Drake,* bringing him a full measure of glory and making him overnight one of the most talked-about, most sought-after personalities in the court circles of Paris.

Formation of the *Bonhomme Richard* Squadron, a joint French-American venture, had required an interminable effort, clogged by delays over diplomatic, supply and personnel problems, and it was still far from being the crack force Jones would have liked. The squadron had been financed almost entirely by the French, and that fact had created a confused situation in the command structure. Though Jones was commodore, his authority was not absolute. At the insistence of the French, the captains of the two frigates, both of them French naval officers holding special American commissions, had retained some vague independence—the ships of the squadron, the agreement specified, were associated together by "common consent." Jones was merely the first among equals, having on all important decisions to consult with his captains. This was an impossible arrangement for the proper conduct of a naval task force, and because of it Jones had very nearly refused his appointment. He had agreed only to avoid wasting more time ashore.

Even his own ship, the *Bonhomme Richard* (named as a compliment to Benjamin Franklin, then minister to France, whose *Poor Richard's Almanac* was just then popular among the French), was not quite the vessel he had hoped for. Thirteen years old and built as a merchantman for the East Indian trade, its brine-soaked planks had been worn and weathered by numerous voyages to China. Its length, about 145 feet, and beam of about 35 feet put it in a class with most English frigates and made it by far the largest ship Jones had yet commanded. On its conversion from merchantman to warship, however, while it was unusually sturdy, it had proved neither a fast sailer nor a nimble handler, especially weighted down as it was by nearly sixty tons of armament.

COMMODORE
JOHN PAUL JONES
Study model for the life-size
statue, by American sculptor
Charles Henry Niehaus,
now standing in Washington, D.C.
(Courtesy U.S. Naval Academy)

CAPT. SIR RICHARD PEARSON
Oil painting by C. Grignion showing Captain Pearson some years
after the battle, when he had been invested with a knighthood.
(*Courtesy National Maritime Museum, London*)

JOHN PAUL JONES
Contemporary gouache drawing, about 1781, by an unknown artist.
The battle is depicted in the lower panel.
(*Courtesy J. P. Morgan Library*)

LT. RICHARD DALE
Engraving from an oil painting by J. Wood, showing Dale a few
years after the battle in the uniform of a captain in the United States
Navy.
(*Courtesy U.S. Naval Academy*)

Gold medal awarded to
John Paul Jones by the
United States Congress in 1782
to commemorate his victory
over the *Serapis*.
(*Courtesy U.S. Naval Academy*

JOHN PAUL JONES
Marble bust executed in 1781 by French sculptor
Jean-Antoine Houdon.
(*Courtesy U.S. Naval Academy*)

Gunports had been cut in the lower decks to accommodate fourteen 12-pounders to a side. One deck below this main battery, in the junior officers' mess along the stern quarters, Jones had made further improvisations, installing six long 18-pounders, three to a side. These were old guns which he had managed to pry loose from the French navy and he was not quite happy with their age or condition. On quarterdeck and forecastle, in addition, there stood six 9-pounders, giving the *Richard* a total armament of forty guns. The force of her twenty-gun broadside was thus a respectable 250 pounds in weight of metal. But the main battery was made up entirely of 12-pounders, some old, some new, and these did not have anywhere near the smashing power of the few eighteens on the deck below. The heavier guns had been known to penetrate several feet of solid oak, well beyond the capability of the twelves.

The working crew of the *Richard* had been recruited in France, where there existed no regular supply of American sailors, and consequently was polyglot in makeup. At the start of the cruise the crew had numbered nearly 150 men, about one-third American. But this total had been reduced by assignments to the various prizes captured along the way, and by some desertions off Ireland (a boatload of men sent in pursuit of the deserters, in charge of the ship's third lieutenant, became lost in a fog and had to land in Ireland, further reducing the *Richard*'s complement). The effective crew was now, at most, perhaps 120, a number barely adequate in a fight to handle both guns and sails. In the main battery alone, the fourteen guns to a side required for proper handling a total of at least seventy men. If the guns on the other side were to be opened up, these men would run across to serve them as well.

A little less than half were Americans, volunteers from among the prisoners who had been exchanged to France from English jails, and who were glad of a chance to return to the fighting. "Revenge," one of them admitted, "sometimes is quite pleasant to men, and we then believed that the said Jones would not disappoint us in our great wish and desire." There was also in the crew a large group of Englishmen, sailors captured at different times by other vessels, who preferred service with the Americans rather than starvation and slow death in some rotting French prison hulk. Jones was not happy about having these men aboard, but they were good hands and there was little else available. If closely watched, he felt, the English volunteers could do no harm and in a fight they could be counted on, since their own country now regarded them as traitors.

Most of the remainder of the crew was made up of Portuguese volunteers, along with a few from Scotland, Sweden, Norway, and the East Indies. Also aboard was a company of French marines, comprising 137 men and officers, some 40 apprentice boys, and a number of landsmen, such as clerks, cooks, stewards, coopers and tailors. And deep in the ship's dimly lit hold, closely confined, were at least one hundred English prisoners, recently taken off captured vessels.

Of the *Bonhomme Richard*'s twenty officers, all were aboard by their own choice. "I wish for none but volunteers," Jones had stipulated, "who with all their hearts are determined to go with me anywhere and everywhere in pursuit of honor." In this, at least, his wish had been granted.

Second in rank to Jones was First Lieutenant Richard Dale, a clever, good-natured young man who in his spirit of enterprise almost equaled Jones himself. Only twenty-two, the Virginia-born Dale had begun the war as a loyalist, actually fighting for a time on the British side. His skull still bore the track of a Yankee musket ball fired from a cutter during a skirmish on the Rappahannock. He came into American hands when his vessel was taken by the armed brig *Lexington,* commanded by the celebrated John Barry. Under Barry's influence, Dale took up the colonials' cause with ardor and joined the *Lexington* as a midshipman.

Later when the *Lexington,* after a fierce, two-hour fight, was captured by an English man-of-war, Dale became a prisoner in notorious Mill Prison, Portsmouth. Eventually he escaped, was recaptured after two weeks of wandering, and for punishment was confined to the dreaded Black Hole—where, to the great annoyance of his jailors, he passed the time loudly singing "rebellious songs." Released from the Hole, he promptly escaped once more and this time was able to smuggle himself to France. Overjoyed to learn that the famous Captain Jones was fitting out an expedition, he eagerly volunteered and was taken on, first as master's mate, later being promoted to first lieutenant. "His bosom now beat high with expectation at the opening of brighter prospects," recorded an early interviewer, as the young officer began dreaming of "a brilliant career of glory."

Ranking third in the chain of command was Lt. Henry Lunt, twenty-six, of Newburyport, Massachusetts, who had been with Jones in the *Providence*. Lunt, too, had spent time languishing in Mill Prison, two long years in fact, but on being exchanged he had immediately presented himself to his old commander. Next came three Irishmen, the only non-Americans among the officers: Sublieutenants Eugene McCarthy, James O'Kelly and Edward Stack. The oldest officer was Matthew Mease, a fifty-year-old Philadelphian in France on government business at the time, who was eager to see some fighting. Mease had gladly accepted the only post left open, that of purser, and had announced himself as ready to take a turn at the guns as well. Dr. Lawrence Brooke, a young Virginian of good family and cultured tastes, was the surgeon. There were also ten midshipmen, all in their late teens or early twenties.

No less than eleven nationalities were represented aboard the *Bonhomme Richard,* and among the ordinary seamen there were many who not only lacked any real naval skills, but who neither spoke nor understood English (about one-third of the original crew came from non-English-speaking nations).

These deficiencies alone, as Lt. Dale later soberly commented, tended "to depress rather than elevate a just hope of success in a combat."

Steadily tacking in the light wind, by one o'clock the *Serapis* had come nearly abreast of Flamborough Head. Now, from high in the foremast, her lookout bellowed down that he had the masts of four ships in sight—distance about fifteen miles, hulls not yet visible.

Progress over the unruffled surface was excruciatingly slow in the zephyr-like breeze, and two more hours of hauling round on short tacks were required before Pearson could observe the strangers plain from his deck. It was indeed a squadron, he saw, though smaller than expected, comprised of one large ship, two frigates and what appeared to be a brig or corvette. All four vessels were advancing bows-on, so nothing could be seen of their armament. The hull of the leader was all black, without any of the usual horizontal striping, but the others seemed to have some red or yellow here and there over the black. All were carrying British colors at the mainmast peak and at the stern—which meant little since, in these waters, Jones would hardly display an American flag. As with all warships cruising hostile territory, he would disguise his real character under friendly colors until the last moment.

By now the convoy was north of the Head once more, in the lee of *Serapis,* though many of the heavily laden ships were still struggling far offshore, victims of the slack winds. Pearson now gave orders to have his ship brought to, and he then ran signal flags aloft calling the *Countess* to come up and join him. Here, if necessary, the two would make their stand against a foe that appeared to be at least double their strength. Then, with the sloop slowly drawing near, the afternoon quiet was suddenly broken as the excited rattle of the war drums began to sound, summoning all hands to battle stations. Up and down the long lengths of the open decks marched the marine drummers, one on each side of the ship, drumsticks whirring in a rapid tattoo.

Below, on the main and lower gun decks, the grim-faced crewmen rushed to gather with their lieutenants, and then dispersed along the line of cannon. The carriage lashings that held the guns secure when not in use were loosened, and the guns run inboard. Barrels, touchholes, sponges, worms and rammers were inspected, water and sand tubs readied, with extra slow fuses fixed around the tub edges, their glowing ends hanging inward. The stacked roundshot were wiped clean, grape, cannister and bar shot loosened for easier handling. From the powder magazine on the orlop deck (the lowest deck before the hold) the first cartridges were brought up in special leather carrying cases, by the powder monkeys. Each cylindrical cartridge bag, made of flannel, held several pounds of highly sensitive black powder.

In the dank, low-ceilinged, dimly lit cockpit (the hospital section, amidships of the orlop deck) the surgeon, William Bannatyne, and his assistants laid out two or three makeshift operating tables, draped with rough cloth or sail, along with bandages, a few crude instruments and tubs of water. Other tubs, ominously empty, stood nearby ready to receive the discarded results of the amputations that were almost inevitable in a sea fight. Spare canvas was laid on the open deck nearby, wherever space was available, to receive the wounded as they were brought down.

Topside, the men hauled up and secured the mainsails on all three masts. If left unfurled in a fight, these lower sails would not only obscure the vision of the fighting men but would quickly be set afire or chewed to pieces by flying shot. The jibs and staysails, topsails and topgallants were left in place, with groups of attentive sailors standing by the braces and sheets, ready on the instant to alter the set and spread of the sails as the captain directed.

Other men clambered about in the rigging, reinforcing with chains and stout ropes the fastenings of the long, heavy yardarms to prevent them from crashing down to the deck if their regular slings should be shot away. Grappling hooks, with lengths of rope attached, were stowed along the bulwarks on the open deck, while hundreds of buckets of water were sluiced along all the decks, and down the passageways, to eliminate any chance that spilled gunpowder might be set off. Casks and tubs of water for dousing fires and long-handled axes for cutting away wreckage were set up at intervals. To the men authorized to have them, pistols, cutlasses and pikes were passed out.

Now the portside batteries were readied, both nines and eighteens. First, the gunports were triced up, bringing daylight streaming into the dark, cramped gun decks. At the command "load!" the loader slipped a powder cartridge into the muzzle and it was rammed in by the second loader, standing opposite. Then a wad was shoved down against the cartridge and finally the heavy iron shot was inserted and rammed home. Since the guns would not be used immediately a second wad was put in to hold the shot in place. Pearson, determined to sell his ship as dearly as possible, had ordered all the guns to be double-shotted (loaded with two rounds apiece), so a second shot and another wad were now rammed in.

"Run out!" came the next command and all hands began hauling on the side tackle (ropes affixed by pulleys to both the gun carriage and the ship's side), slowly drawing the ponderous wheeled carriage forward until its front edge touched the port sill, with its muzzle protruding through the side. At "prime!" the crew's chief took a thin wire from his belt and poked it down through the narrow vent in the cannon's breech, piercing the flannel cartridge. Removing the wire, he inserted a thin fuse into the vent and stepped back. A slow match touched to this fuse would discharge the gun in less than a second.

On both the *Serapis* and the *Countess,* though there was much hurrying about, much shouting of orders, questions and replies, all preparations were undertaken with a minimum of confusion. Directives bawled out by the bosun and his mates, the master at arms and the chief gunners were loud, clear, familiar from long practice, and were crisply obeyed. By about 6 P.M., just as the bright day was changing to dull gray in the east, Captain Pearson was informed that his ship was battle ready.

It wouldn't be much of a battle, he thought as he fixed his eyes on the tall sails growing against the slate-colored skies to the south. The three larger vessels were still bows-on, concealing their armament, reason enough for suspicion. Assuming the least, Pearson reasoned, each of the large ships might be carrying fifteen guns to a side, perhaps a mixture of nines and twelves. If the enemy formed Line of Battle, as he almost certainly would, then the *Serapis* could expect to receive, on a single pass of the line, the full force of at least forty-five cannon, the three ships combined throwing perhaps 500 pounds in weight of metal. In this light breeze, the first pass of the line might occupy, say, seven or eight minutes, allowing some two minutes for each ship to come up, deliver its broadside and pass on.

To the first ship Pearson could return a full broadside, but he probably would not be able to reload in time to retaliate fully on the second ship. When the third came alongside, the *Serapis's* firepower would have been much reduced, perhaps drastically, if the American gunners proved at all competent. A second pass by Jones's line might very well put an end to the battle, especially if the line were to be curved around the *Serapis* for raking fire (a consecutive broadside into stern or bow, the hail of shot passing the length of the ship and doing execution as if it were a scythe). Elapsed time for the two passes could be as brief as one glass, a half hour.

Should his rigging and sails remain reasonably intact, Pearson might hold out longer by taking evasive action. But then he would lay himself more open to repeated raking, which would seriously, and perhaps to little purpose, increase his casualties. The *Countess,* with her small battery of ten 6-pounders on a side, could make little or no difference in the outcome. An hour seemed the limit of time, in any case, to which Pearson could hope to extend the fight and delay the American. But by then the last of the scrambling merchantmen should have found a haven.

Pearson now performed one last act of preparation. He ordered the flagstaff at the ship's stern taken down, with its huge Red Ensign, and he called for a hammer and nails. The ensign was removed from the loose halyards; then its inner edge was nailed directly to the staff. When the staff was once more in place on the stern, the Red Ensign ruffling lazily in the slight breeze, word of the captain's action went through the ship. No man had to ask what it meant.

From the *Richard*'s poop deck Captain Jones observed with disgust that the lone ship was not coming off her port tack to continue southward, but instead was reaching back north, toward the land, no doubt making for Bridlington. Long before the *Richard* could come up with her, she would be riding safely at anchor.

Then from aloft there came an excited shout and Jones's heart soared. Convoy ahead! Bearing north-northeast, about fifteen miles. Ten, a dozen, twenty sail in sight!

His voice now far from soft, Jones started issuing orders and all along the deck men began hauling on ropes. Rapidly the royal yards were swayed up, the studding sails unfurled. Signal flags were hoisted ordering the squadron into a General Chase. Two guns were shot off to recall Lt. Lunt and his boatload of men—though Jones did not intend to lose precious moments waiting, and it was questionable whether the lieutenant could get back in time. Lunt immediately brought the pilot boat about, but before many minutes, though he kept up his pursuit of the receding *Richard,* he saw with dismay that he would be left behind.

Lt. Dale, who had been on watch the night before and was asleep in his cabin, came abruptly awake with the noise and activity above. He rushed up, still dressing, his blood quickening with the news that worthy prey was in the offing. His visions of the glory that awaited, however, were blotted out with a rush at Jones's curt order to have the ship cleared for action.

There was now hardly enough wind to belly the *Richard*'s sails, but it was still blowing from the southwest, so Jones and his consorts were able to make the most of it. The four ships were running almost due north, with the fast-sailing *Alliance* gradually forging ahead on the *Richard*'s starboard. During the first hour's run, more and more sails came into view, until it seemed to the lookout that there must be at least thirty of them.

Jones himself, with mounting elation, now felt certain that he was at last in pursuit of one of the supreme opportunities for which he had long hungered, the chance to swoop down on one of England's important Baltic convoys. If he could succeed in breaking it up, smashing some of the ships to the bottom, taking others as prizes, then he could indeed return home to France in triumph. All the frustrations of his disappointing six weeks' prowl would be wiped out. Of course, there would be an armed escort to encounter, but with two frigates in support, that should present no problem. Among the three of them, he had at his command over one hundred guns.

The *Pallas* was armed with thirty-two cannon, mostly 9-pounders, and was ably commanded by Captain Denis-Nicolas Cottineau. The *Alliance,* American-built, was nearly the equal of the *Richard* in her armament, carrying a total of thirty-six guns, most of them 12-pounders. Unfortunately, however, her captain, forty-two-year-old Pierre Landais, instead of giving wholehearted support to Jones, had proved to be a source of serious discord. An officer of seasoned knowledge and personal charm when not under stress, when in command of a vessel at sea, as Jones soon learned, Landais became strangely harsh and unpredictable. He had been granted his commission directly from the United States Congress, and he had lost no time in taking arrogant advantage of the fact, and of the vague nature of Jones's command.

Several times during the cruise, Landais had bluntly disagreed with the commodore's direction of the squadron and had sailed off on his own to hunt for prizes, returning when it suited him. Rudely outspoken, regarded as a bothersome eccentric by his fellow officers, even perhaps a bit mad, on more than one occasion he had not hesitated to reply to Jones's orders in grossly disrespectful, even insolent terms. Jones, hampered by his diluted authority, and rather than upset the squadron's arrangements while at sea, had held his temper—which could be ferocious—and had repeatedly overlooked the Frenchman's erratic conduct. But he no longer wholly trusted him.

After another hour's run the convoy's escort

was identified: a frigate and a sloop lying to on the water, about ten miles distant, waiting.

Making scarcely three knots in the fitful breeze, the *Richard* glided sluggishly ahead, and it was after five o'clock, with graying skies reducing visibility, before Jones was able to count the frigate's armament. Noting her two covered gun decks and her battery of 18-pounders in the lower tier, he finally became aware of the formidable opponent he was rushing to attack.

At about six he saw that the enemy frigate had begun to move. It was standing inshore, followed at a distance by the sloop. Accordingly, though the frigate's purpose was unclear, Jones altered his own course slightly, to a northwest heading. Perhaps, he thought, the Englishman was prudently declining battle in the face of the odds, leaving the convoy to make the best of its way ashore. If so, Jones determined, he would force battle upon her. He was not going to lose the glory of taking a fifty-gun frigate.

The staccato roll of the war drums rattled along the *Richard*'s length and all over the ship men began hurrying to battle stations. Up to the foretop —the fighting platform of the foremast situated some forty feet above the deck—went fourteen men under command of a midshipman. Lt. Stack, leading a mixed force of twenty sailors and marines, scrambled up the rigging to the mainmast platform, while another midshipman took nine men with him into the mizzen top. A squad of twenty French marines, with muskets, grenades and coehorns, trooped to its station on the poop deck, other marines dispersed to the forecastle and amidships, the rest stayed in reserve below.

Lt. Dale, who would command the main battery of 12-pounders, assembled the seventy men of his gun crews on the lower deck. Those who would serve the three big 18-pounders, about twenty men in all, gathered round the chief gunner, one deck below the twelves. The starboard gunports fluttered open and the muzzles of all seventeen belowdeck guns slowly emerged through the ship's side as the men hauled on the tackle. On forecastle and quarterdeck, the 9-pounders were also shotted and ready. Here and there on deck other men hauled on the running rigging, clewing up the mainsails and reinforcing the heavy yardarms with chain.

Jones now ordered signal made to his two consorts—a combination of blue and yellow flags on all three masts—to form Line of Battle. Obediently, the *Pallas* trailed in astern of the *Richard*. The *Alliance,* however, instead of falling back to take her position at the rear of *Pallas,* acted in a way for which no one was prepared. She hauled her wind and sheered off to the northeast, apparently heading for open water. *Vengeance,* too small to have a place in the line, kept her distance.

Perplexed, his anger rising, Jones saw that Landais had either misunderstood or ignored his signals, but there was nothing to be done about the apparent defection in these last critical moments. Then, in deepening consternation, he observed that the *Pallas,* too, had begun to drop off astern. In minutes she was out of the line and had altered course to the northeast. The *Richard,* within a half mile of its target, was on its own.

Jones wasted no time in trying to fathom the motives of his two captains, nor did he give any thought to avoiding the powerful enemy frigate until he could form up his line again. He would initiate the attack himself, trusting that the other two would join in when able. If necessary, he was ready to engage entirely on his own—though it was now evident, to even the rawest seaman aboard the *Richard,* that the foe held superiority not only in firepower but quite evidently in her sailing qualities, and very likely in the training of her crew.

It was now about 7 P.M. and the gap between the two ships was steadily diminishing. In the fast-gathering dusk, land, sea and sky were sweepingly blended in one leaden hue. The quiet heavens hung unclouded, the surface of the water lay perfectly smooth, without billow or swell, "even as in a millpond." Along the two hulls the neat rows of square gunports glowed menacingly in the light of lanterns. Low to the north an early moon displayed a brightening silver disk. It would be a harvest moon.

Slowly rounding to on the portside of the frigate, Jones took up the same westerly heading. He could have chosen to open the battle on either side of the enemy, but he accepted the weather gauge—to windward—his usual preference in a fight. The position would give him a slight advantage in maneuvering, and the breeze, such as it was, would carry away from his ship the dense clouds of smoke thrown up by the guns.

Both vessels were now pointed straight for Flamborough Head, which lay some three miles distant. As the bow of Jones's ship drew even with the stern of the Englishman, the two were about fifty yards apart and closing.

Captain Pearson, at his stern rail, noted the scattering of the three strangers—the two frigates far off his stern and standing north, the remaining ship rapidly drawing up—and was puzzled by it. Perhaps the first two had been sent in pursuit of the convoy, leaving only a single ship to engage the escort. But that hardly made sense, since the vessel now bearing down was essentially a one-decker whose main armament appeared to be 12-pounders. Of course, the other ships might easily return, but at the moment it seemed that the engagement was not to commence with a devastating Line of Battle. Or was it possible, after all, that these were not the ships of John Paul Jones?

Pearson spoke to his first lieutenant, John Wright. Raising a speaking trumpet to his mouth and pointing it at the *Richard,* Lt. Wright hailed loudly, "What ship is that?"

The answer floated back over the water and was clearly heard: "The *Princess Royal*."

Again Wright hailed, "Where from?" A shout came back from the other vessel, but this time the words were unintelligible.

Pearson spoke a second time to his lieutenant, who once more shouted through the trumpet, framing his words with care: "Where from? Reply instantly or I shall be under the necessity of firing into you."

In the fading light Pearson and his officers waited, each man counting the seconds. Aloft on the fighting platforms, crowded along the bulwarks, below at the guns, over three hundred other men also waited, straining to listen. But no answer came. There was only the low sighing of the wind and the steady murmur of rushing water as it curled in foam along the ponderous bows of the two ships.

2

The Battle

John Paul Jones stood immobile on his quarter-deck as the *Bonhomme Richard,* edging to starboard, bore steadily down on the British frigate. Nearby stood his young aides, Midshipmen John Linthwaite and John Mayrant. Just behind, in charge of the two 9-pounders along the starboard quarter, with their four-man crews, was the middle-aged man who had been so eager for action, purser Matthew Mease. All gazed fixedly at the smoothly gliding frigate, now separated from them by scarcely a hundred feet of open water.

To the several inquiries from the *Serapis,* Jones had replied personally, a speaking trumpet to his mouth. In answer to the second hail, anxious to gain time so that the gap between the ships might be reduced as much as possible, he had deliberately responded with gibberish. When the third hail came, with its ultimatum, he did not bother to answer. Instead, he gave Midshipman Linthwaite two orders, to be carried out simultaneously: haul down the British ensign and break out American colors—commence firing, full broadsides.

Speedily the command was relayed to Mease, then by men stationed at the hatchways to Lt. Dale on the lower deck, down to the chief gunner who stood ready with the eighteens, and forward to the man handling the single nine on the forecastle. Seconds later, as American flags blossomed at mainmast and stern, the *Richard*'s starboard side erupted. A sharp reverberating roar, echoing over the water, shattered the evening calm as livid flame leaped from the cannon mouths and swirling billows of yellow-gray smoke rose on the breeze. Slowly the rising smoke blended into one large pall and drifted upwind to envelop the target.

The gun carriages, recoiling, rolled abruptly backward until they were checked by the breeching tackle, with the gun muzzles just inside the ports. Working smoothly, the crewmen jammed the long-handled sponges into the smoking barrels to swab away any residue, then rammed home in succession fresh cartridges, wads and shot. Even as the men began hauling on the side tackle to run the muzzles once more through the ports, the guns were being primed.

Almost at the same moment that the *Richard* had fired, the *Serapis*'s broadside had also thundered out in flame and smoke and the fifty shot from her twenty-five double-shotted guns, invisible in their hurtling velocity, smashed with terrible impact into the *Richard*'s length. Crashing and thudding against the hull, many of the larger shot plunged through the wood and exploded large, jagged splinters into the air, two or three of them blasting ragged holes just at or below the waterline. Throughout the ship, as the tension broke, exulting shouts and howls arose. Here and there, choking, shrieking men crumpled or were hurled, torn and bloodied, to the deck, flesh ripped by iron or pierced by thick, flying splinters. In the topsails, rips and holes appeared and several of the braces parted and fell snakelike through the air. Deep within the ship, paying little attention to the excitement around them, the carpenter and his yeomen hurried along the orlop deck carrying shot plugs (cone-shaped pieces of wood covered with oakum) and other materials to repair the leaks.

Again the guns of both ships thundered out, again almost simultaneously. Aboard the *Richard*, however, there was a second, echolike explosion which followed immediately on its broadside, the sound rumbling up from deep within the stern section. The crowded, low-ceilinged junior officers' mess, where the 18-pounders were mounted, was in chaos, filled with dense clouds of blinding smoke, through which there licked tongues of searing flame. The explosion had not been caused by the hail of fire from the *Serapis,* but by the accidental bursting, on the second discharge, of two of the old guns, with a number of extra powder cartridges also being set off. Sprawled on the deck there lay a dozen men, some unmoving, others writhing and groaning with their wounds and burns. The survivors stumbled about choking and gasping as they groped blindly for the hatchway. The devastating force of the blast, it was soon found, had also wrecked part of the deck overhead, dismounting two of the 12-pounders.

When the details of the disaster reached Jones on the quarterdeck, he unhesitatingly ordered the rest of the eighteens abandoned and the ports closed. Though the loss of four guns represented a severe depletion in his armament, and though he could ill afford to give up the remaining eighteens—with some effort they could have been trundled across to replace the damaged ones—he had quickly judged that the risk of another accident with the aged cannon outweighed any possible gain.

Even as Jones was giving his orders, the *Serapis* delivered her third broadside, the shot crashing with devastating accuracy through the bulwarks, tearing up planking, slicing through sails and rigging, killing and wounding men, especially among the marines on the exposed poop deck. Nearly half of the twenty marines went down, and the others were ordered to leave the poop and spread for cover in the ship's waist.

The battle had barely begun, Jones thought, and already the enemy had made his superiority felt. With the *Richard*'s main battery reduced to a dozen guns, some of the important mainsail braces shot away, several holes below the waterline which could not be quite plugged up, and some twenty men killed or wounded out of an already inadequate crew, it was starkly clear to Jones that he could not survive for long in a steady cannonade. Nor could he take the risk of a raking, now a definite threat since the *Richard*'s maneuverability had been impaired. Even one raking broadside, pouring in at stern or bow, might easily mow down half the crew. The disheartening effects of this, along with the damage, could very well end the fight.

Looking round over his stern, Jones saw that neither of his consorts was making an effort to rejoin. The *Pallas* appeared to be trying to close with the British sloop but the smaller vessel was maintaining a safe distance. What Captain Landais in the *Alliance* might have in mind, Jones found it hard to discern—at the moment he was contentedly trailing after the *Pallas* as if enjoying an afternoon's excursion.

Jones had two choices. He could break off, retire to a distance, and wait for help. Or he could carry the fight to the enemy and try to take her by boarding. The first course would be the safer and under normal circumstances the correct one. But then the Englishman might decide to break off too, and run for the shore. The second choice would be an obvious gamble, and a desperate one, since it would allow Jones only a single thrust at his opponent's vitals. If that failed, then all would be lost. Still, he had over a hundred well-trained marines, and nearly a hundred seamen. If he could succeed in placing even a part of this force on the enemy's decks, the battle could at least be fought on more equal terms.

To Sailing Master Samuel Stacey, standing close at hand, Jones gave his orders: Place the *Richard* alongside the frigate, to starboard, in a position to grapple. They were going to board. To another aide he gave further instructions, to be relayed to the men on the fighting platforms: Concentrate fire on the opposing topmen, not on the decks—clear out the enemy's sharpshooters so that the boarders would not be under a rain of musketry and grenades.

At a word from Stacey, the *Richard's* fore and main topsails were backed (turned so that the wind caught their fronts and acted as a brake) and the ship slowly dropped astern of the *Serapis*. Then, a few seconds later, as the English ship was cleared, Stacey called for the sails to be filled again, with the helm aweather. Her bow swinging to the right, so that the *Serapis's* black-and-yellow hull for a moment lay dead ahead, the *Richard* surged forward. Except for a few muskets, since neither ship could now bring a cannon to bear, all firing had ceased.

A long minute passed, then two, then three, then Stacey ordered the helm put over, alee, and the bow swung heavily back to the left. But Captain Pearson, anticipating the movement, put his own helm alee and brought his stern into the *Richard*'s path. At this, Jones shouted for the wheel to be held hard over. He would go alongside the enemy's port instead of starboard.

It was too late. There was not enough room to pass. Bearing swiftly down, the *Richard*'s starboard bow crunched hollowly against the frigate's port quarter to the sound of grinding, tearing wood. A hundred muskets crackled, sputtering grenades flew through the air to thump and roll and explode on both decks, grappling hooks leaped out from the *Richard*'s bulwarks, some snagging a hold here and there on the Englishman only to be cut loose by axe-wielders. A few boarders, brandishing pikes and cutlasses, started to clamber up on the *Richard*'s bowsprit ready to drop to the other deck. Jones, however, gave abrupt orders to haul the ship off. No boarding attempt, he knew, could succeed across such a narrow point of access. The sails were backed and the American dropped clear.

Captain Pearson on his quarterdeck watched closely as his foe receded. At the same time he noticed that the wind on her backed sails was shoving her head round toward the north. Now he had his chance. If he could throw the *Serapis* to starboard quickly enough, he should be able to go down across the enemy's forefoot. Well placed, one raking broadside slamming into her bow might end the battle. Incredibly, he thought, he might yet be able to save his ship from the scattered squadron of the Yankee pirate, might even be able to leave one of them crippled and unfit for further mischief.

To his aide, Pearson calmly gave the order to take the ship across the enemy's advancing bow. At the same time he sent a messenger hurrying below to inform the battery lieutenant that they would shortly have a target. The guns were not to be fired together, he cautioned, but each must wait until it was brought to bear squarely in a line with the enemy's entire length. The pass would occupy perhaps a minute, with the forward guns firing first. Despite the fact that several of the *Serapis*'s cannon had been dismounted, and several men had been killed or wounded, Pearson was confident that he still possessed sufficient force to gut the American from sternpost to cutwater. The helmsman obediently swung the large wheel.

As the *Serapis* veered sharply right, she brought the wind more nearly over her stern. Now with sails straining directly before the breeze, she pointed her bows to intercept the *Richard*'s path. This time, however, it was Pearson who was foiled. Jones, anticipating him, had also altered course. He was now coming left, perhaps hoping to deliver a raking by the stern, perhaps merely trying to find open water. Pearson spoke again to his lieutenant, the wheel was put over, and the *Serapis* turned briskly away to port—"wore short round upon her heel," as Lt. Dale described it.

For a brief moment as the two bows swung in opposite directions, some of the *Serapis*'s gunners had a target and a dozen guns boomed out in rapid succession, several scoring hits across less than a hundred feet of water. Then the Englishman straightened up and was once again pointed on a line with Flamborough Head, a little north of west.

Pearson's deft countermove had taken Jones by surprise. Before he could order a correction, he saw that he would again be aboard the enemy, this time bow to stern, and nearly in a straight line. With a loud clumping sound, the *Richard* ran into the other ship, smashing some of the glass windows of the rear cabins and splintering the elaborate carvings on the stern galleries. At the same time, her jib boom carried in over the *Serapis*'s stern railing. Again the muskets volleyed furiously. The cannon of both ships, once more unable to bear, remained silent. Like an old fighter, out of breath and grateful for the chance to rest in a clinch even for fleeting seconds, the *Richard* leaned heavily on her younger opponent. Then Jones backed the sails and hauled off astern—but almost immediately he gave the order to fill.

Slowly the *Richard* ranged up on the *Serapis*'s portside, resuming the weather gauge, while the Englishman's after guns, deflected left, flashed and thundered. Captain Pearson, impatient to bring the whole weight of his broadside into action, now backed his topgallants in order to check his speed a little and allow his opponent to come up faster. In moments, the two ships were abeam, bow-and-bow, with less than a hundred feet of water between them. The English gunners, firing at will as fast as they could reload, set up a relentless cannonading and almost without ceasing roundshot and bar shot smashed into the *Richard*'s hull, decks, masts, rigging and sails. It was a rain of devastation that no ship could bear for long.

On his quarterdeck Jones waited, his eyes fixed on the other ship's bow, which was still dropping back. He would make his move at just the right moment, when his sails were positioned to blanket those of the enemy, momentarily taking the wind out of them. Suddenly he felt the breeze freshening. This was an unexpected gift of fate which had come at precisely the right instant. To the sailing master he snapped an order: "Athwart hawse, Mr. Stacey. Lay the enemy on board!"

Stacey immediately barked instructions to the helmsman, and the wheel spun rapidly, throwing the ship in a tight circle to the right. If sails and helm responded smartly, the *Richard* would pass lengthwise in front of her opponent, and would receive the onrushing bow against her own side, amidships (the two forming a capital T). While grappling, the American could deliver raking broadsides, at the same time sweeping the forecastle with muskets and grenades in preparation for boarding. And in that position the *Serapis* would be relatively helpless, unable to return even one gun.

Within less than a minute the *Richard* had squared herself across the path of the oncoming frigate, though with not quite the precision that Jones had intended, since some of the mainsail braces had been shot away and the ship had answered the abrupt change of course sluggishly. Still, as the *Serapis*'s bow loomed larger and larger, her long, outreaching jib boom slicing through the air as if it were a thrown spear, it seemed that the gamble would succeed.

But instead of meeting her adversary amidships, the *Serapis* swung precipitately to her left. With speed unslackened, she ran heavily into the *Richard*'s starboard quarter, her jib boom thrusting far over the poop deck and in among the mizzen shrouds—another few feet, another few seconds, and the Englishman would have sailed clear of the *Richard*'s stern, in a perfect position to rake. Both ships trembled violently under the shock of the collision and high on the *Serapis*'s fighting platforms the topmen held tight as the masts swayed wildly. "Well done, my brave lads," shouted Jones to those around him on the quarterdeck, "we have got her now!"

The position of the two ships, however—linked roughly as a broad V—was not the best possible one for the American. It exposed his whole side to the enemy's formidable starboard battery. Though these guns had not yet been used and the ports were still closed, it was certain that Pearson was even now giving the order to unlimber them. And the point of contact, as before, was a narrow one, which would make very doubtful any attempt to board. Yet Jones, aware that he might not be given another chance, determined to hang on. There would be no more backing off for either ship. One or the other must triumph. And if victory was to go to the Englishman, Jones vowed grimly, it would be only with the surface of the North Sea washing over the deck of the *Bonhomme Richard.*

Even as he made his decision, Jones grabbed at one end of a line that had been jerked loose from the *Serapis*'s jib and was trailing at his feet. He pulled it taut, took a turn on a mizzen cleat and tied it fast. At the same time he shouted to Master Stacey to rouse out a hawser and lash the enemy jib to the mizzenmast. Stacey disappeared and came back a few moments later carrying a thick coil of rope. In his excitement he was cursing loudly. "It is no time for swearing now, Mr. Stacey," Jones admonished lightly, "you may by the next moment be in eternity!" As he helped with the hawser he added more quietly, "But let us do our duty."

Almost immediately after the collision Pearson had backed his sails in an effort to pull himself free. He was now fully aware of Jones's intention to board, and this was the one thing he wished to prevent. While confident that he stood at least an equal

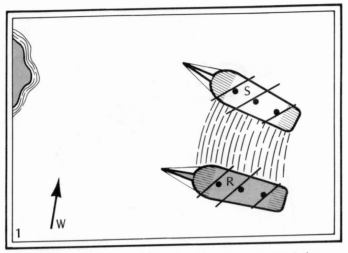

1. Broadside to broadside, sailing toward Flamborough Head, the two ships open fire almost simultaneously.

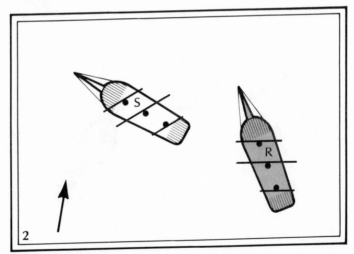

2. Jones drops back and swings north, intending to grapple Pearson's starboard side in order to board the foe.

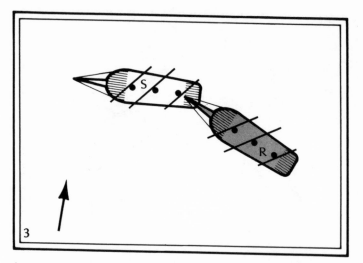

3. Pearson turns away from Jones's grappling attempt, and the swinging ships accidentally collide.

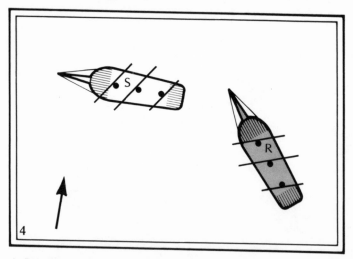

4. Jones drops off, swinging north, while Pearson also turns north hoping to deliver a raking by the bow.

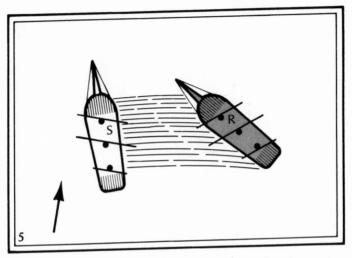

5. With Pearson swinging northeast, Jones comes southwest, intending to rake the Englishman by the stern.

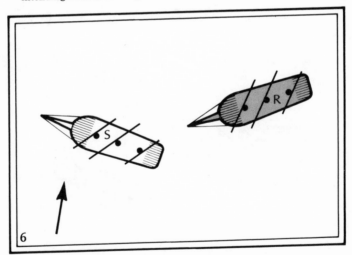

6. Pearson turns west to avoid Jones's raking fire, while Jones continues to swing toward the southwest.

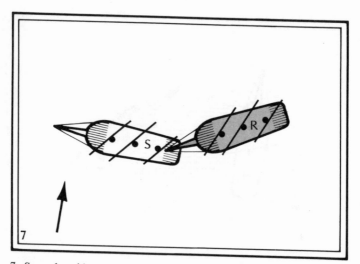

7. Second accidental collision occurs when Jones fails to clear his opponent's stern.

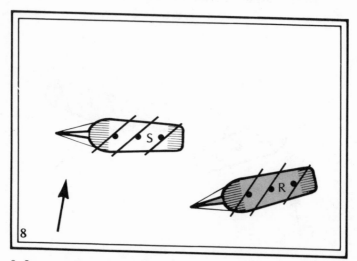

8. Jones ranges up on Pearson's port side in an effort to take the weather gauge.

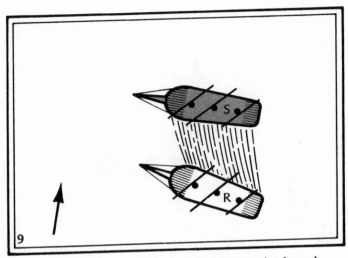

9. Pearson drops back to engage alongside his oncoming foe and broadsiding is resumed.

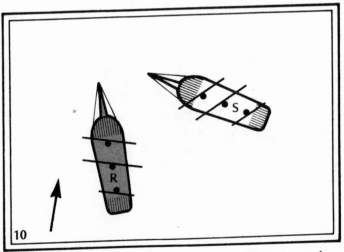

10. Jones swings north across his opponent's bow, hoping to grapple and board.

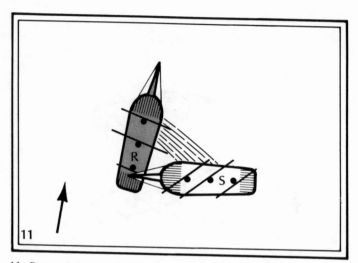

11. Pearson's bow sprit fouls Jones's mizzen shrouds as the two ships collide.

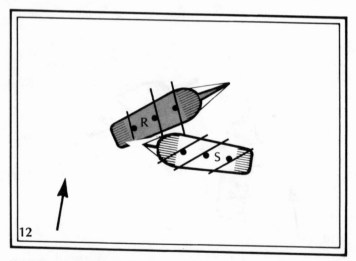

12. Pearson's bow sprit is broken off as the ships, moved by wind and tide, swing together.

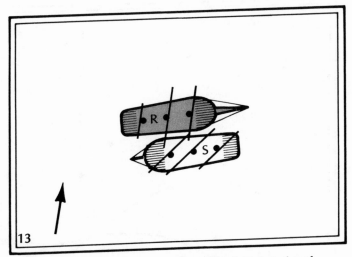

13. Pearson's starboard anchor, in place, fouls Jones's starboard quarter, while Jones orders grappling hooks away.

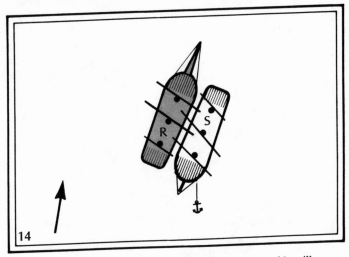

14. Pearson drops his port anchor hoping the wind and tide will separate the ships, but they remain locked together.

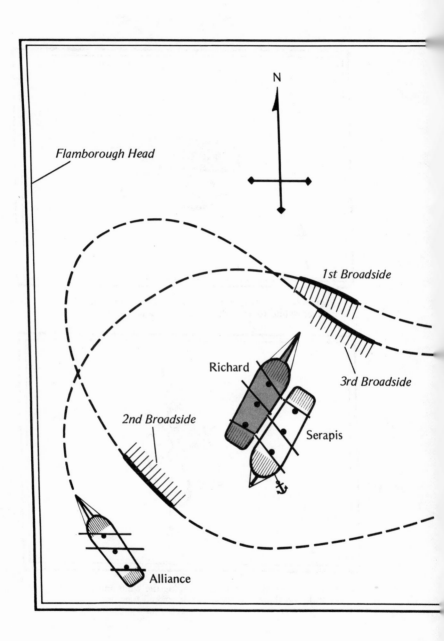

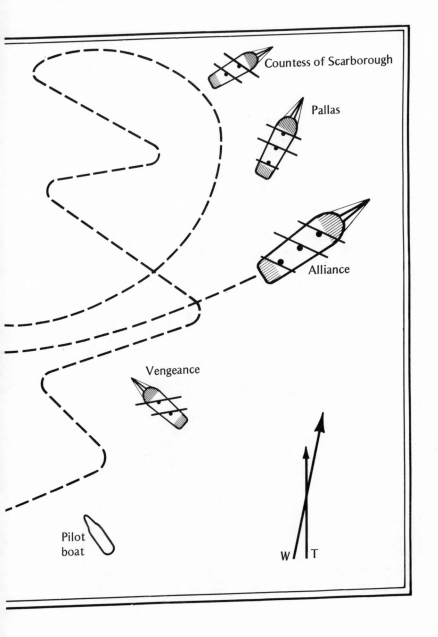

Countess of Scarborough

Pallas

Alliance

Vengeance

Pilot
boat

W T

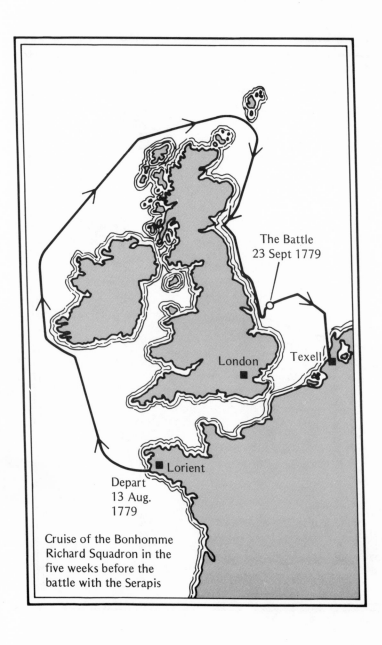

The Battle
23 Sept 1779

London

Texell

Lorient

Depart
13 Aug.
1779

Cruise of the Bonhomme
Richard Squadron in the
five weeks before the
battle with the Serapis

chance in a hand-to-hand melée, he logically pre-ferred to fight from a position of strength, standing off and cannonading until he had reduced his antag-onist to a drifting hulk. But the *Serapis* would not pull clear. She was, apparently, fouled in the other ship's mizzen shrouds, Pearson concluded, with the headsail braces contributing to the tangle.

A loud cracking sound brought Pearson's head up and he saw that the tip of the jib, where it met the *Richard*'s mizzen, had broken off. Then he no-ticed something else, more alarming—the gap be-tween the two ships was diminishing. The wind was pushing him sideways, closing the V. They would soon be touching, side to side. Hastily, Pearson called for the starboard guns to be run out, and then, in a last effort to free himself, he called quickly for the port anchor to be dropped. With the *Serapis* held in place by its anchor, the action of the wind and tide together might wrench the other vessel loose.

Gradually the two ships converged, the *Richard*'s remaining 12-pounders all the while roar-ing above the cacophony of musketry, swivel cannon and coehorns from the fighting tops and the decks of both sides. The *Serapis*'s starboard gunports were still unopened when her whole starboard length crunched roughly against the *Richard*'s hull. The two floated apart a few feet, then pressed together again, this time with their long, outreaching yard-arms noisily entangling, the foresail and mainsail of one to the main and fore of the other.

Dozens of grappling hooks leaped out from the American, tumbling and clattering, then catching, on the *Serapis*'s decks, bulwarks and in the rigging. Pearson shouted for them to be cast off or the lines cut, but every man who rushed to obey was peppered by musket fire and many fell. Then a report was brought to Pearson which told him that the grapnels, on or off, made no difference. The *Serapis*'s other anchor, hanging in its place on the starboard bow, had come afoul of the *Richard*'s stern, the big, curving fluke hooking strongly into the wood. There was no way to break it loose. Bow to stern, the ships were locked inseparably.

With the lower parts of their hulls rudely chafing, the two vessels lay together. Some of the *Richard*'s smoking gun muzzles banged hard against the *Serapis*'s sides and were shoved back inboard, scattering their crewmen. Because of the tumble-home (the inward slope in the upper part of a ship's side) the respective railings were still separated by about ten feet of open space. Pivoting on her payed-out anchor cable, the *Serapis* swung her head into the wind, carrying the *Richard* with her through a half-circle. At last the two came uneasily to rest on a north-south axis.

The starboard guns of the English frigate were now primed and ready. But it was found that most of the gunports, blocked by the crowding of the foe's hull, could not be opened. There was room to swing most of them up only a few inches. Through the bedlam of noise came the loud command of the battery lieutenants: "Blow off the ports!" Deep, echoing thunder and biting smoke filled the *Serapis*'s gun decks as the nines and eighteens, most of them double-shotted, disintegrated their own gunport covers, the hurtling shot crashing on through to the vessel opposite.

Less than three miles away, off the American's portside, rose the shadowy eminence of Flamborough Head. Its grassy level now accommodated more than a thousand spectators, and the crowd continued to swell with excited newcomers as news of the extraordinary sea fight, so close to land, spread through the surrounding towns. From Beverley, Bridlington, Hackness, Filey, Reighton, Burton Agnes, Driffield and Hilderthorpe, men and boys, even many women, afoot, in carriages or on horseback, streamed along the roads, drawn by the wildfire rumor that the pirate Paul Jones had been cornered.

Congregating on the beaches, the piers, any available hill or eminence, all peered breathlessly through the night at the radiant sulphur-cloud that painted the darkness with a myriad of glowing colors. There were even some spectators, those with houses near the shore, who were able to watch the battle from the comfort of their own living rooms. One Scarborough man described how "Thursday evening we were told that there was an engagement at sea. I immediately threw up the sash of the room I was in, and we had a fair view of the engagement, which appeared very severe, for the firing was frequently so quick that we could scarce count the shots."

Since the opening of the battle nearly an hour had passed. It was now full dark and across the blackened waters there fell the glistening track of the bright harvest moon, beaming its placid light from high over the eastern horizon. Palely it tinged with shifting silver the mountainous pall of flame-rent smoke that swelled around the combatants.

The *Countess of Scarborough,* commanded by Captain Thomas Piercy, had not managed to elude her pursuers altogether. While Jones and Pearson were engaged in their strenuous maneuvering, the slow-moving *Pallas* had finally brought the *Countess* to bay, firing broadsides at a distance of several hundred feet. Piercy, though under the muzzles of sixteen guns, had stood his ground and bravely replied with his own small battery of ten 6-pounders. He had no intention, however, of engaging the far more powerful frigate to a finish. That would have been suicide, particularly when there was a second enemy ship standing by, ready at any moment to add its guns to those of the *Pallas.* Even while a hail of shot crashed in on him, Piercy's one insistent thought was to rush to the aid of his commander.

After delivering two or three broadsides, the

Pallas dropped momentarily astern, and Piercy moved quickly to take advantage of the lull. Piling on sail, he tacked south toward the *Serapis*, his progress maddeningly slow in the slight breeze. At a distance of about fifty yards from the battle scene he passed around the two locked ships preparing to attack on the American's off side. But then, in sudden dismay, he realized that there was no certain way to tell the two vessels apart. They were "so close together, and covered with smoke," he later explained, "that I could not distinguish one ship from the other." In the flicker and glare—rolling shadows rapidly alternating with scintillating brightness, shafts of light glancing off the darkened waters and through the swirling curtain of smoke—even the yellow stripes that might have identified the sides of the English ship were disguised.

Unable to fire, hoping that the obscuring veil might lift if even for a moment, Piercy hovered in the vicinity. Instead of lifting, as the big guns continued to roar, the boiling smoke-cloud thickened, lit at its turbulent center by the flashing of cannon, and by the dancing flames that had begun to lick along the touching sides. Then Piercy became aware that the *Pallas,* her shadowy pyramid of sail looming against the moonlight, was again bearing down on him. Rapidly he brought the *Countess* about to meet the renewed threat, and then, in order to draw the American away from the main battle, he pointed his bow due north. His only role, now, he realized, was to occupy his pursuer for as long as he could, and at as great a distance as possible from the *Serapis*.

With the *Countess* pulling away to the north, another, smaller craft emerged from the darkness to the south as Lt. Lunt made his belated appearance on the scene. At once he and the men with him in the pilot boat found themselves amid great confusion.

Drawing up, Lunt observed the luminous cloud that enveloped the vague forms of the two embattled ships, caught a glimpse of the *Pallas* in full pursuit of another vessel, observed the *Alliance* idly hove-to about a mile to windward (southwest) of the battle-cloud, and noticed the *Vengeance* sitting quietly a little to the east, also apparently a mere spectator. One of the ships in the smoke-cloud must be the *Richard*, Lunt knew, and she was obviously locked in a death struggle with her opponent. But why, he wondered, was the *Alliance* standing aside? If she were to engage, then certainly the Englishman must soon surrender.

Lunt's own duty, he was aware, called for him at all hazards to place himself and his fifteen men back aboard the *Richard*. This he was prepared to do, even though he would risk being blown out of the water by the Englishman's big guns, or mistakenly shot at in the darkness and confusion by his own comrades. Yet it might make more sense, he reasoned, if he were to take his men aboard the *Vengeance* and bring that vessel, small and lightly armed as she was, into the action. Her crew numbered nearly seventy hands and she carried half a dozen 4-pounders to a side, a feeble battery yet superior to muskets. If he still could not get aboard the *Richard,* then the corvette might lend some aid to Jones by harrying the enemy's bow and stern, where she would be relatively safe from the big guns.

Running up alongside the *Vengeance,* Lunt talked from his deck with the corvette's captain, Lt. Philip Ricot, explaining his plan. He was surprised to hear that officer flatly refuse to enter the fight. Ricot would not risk his ship when he could provide no real assistance. He would stand by, instead, ready to respond when and where he could be of most use as the battle progressed. But, he insisted, Lunt must make all haste to put himself and his men back aboard the flagship. And for that, the pilot boat was sufficient. Disappointed, more than a little disgusted, but without authority to insist, Lunt came about and sailed west toward the battle-cloud.

Nerves taut, his blood racing in his eagerness to be at his post, some ten minutes later Lunt pulled up to within fifty yards of the fight—and was promptly forced to admit that any attempt to enter blindly into that fiery pandemonium would be courting disaster. Faced with the same heavy pall of smoke that had baffled Piercy, he could not even be sure which ship was his own. Reluctantly he had the pilot boat hove-to. He would await a clearing of the smoke and go aboard when he judged the time was right.

A few minutes later, looking over his portside,

Lunt felt his heart leap with relief and excitement. The tall-masted *Alliance* had at last begun to move. She appeared to be heading straight for the battle.

"Unremitting fury" were the words in which Captain Jones later described the fighting during the first hour or so after the *Serapis* and the *Richard* locked together. The phrase is no exaggeration.

So far, the Englishman had lost only one of the ten big guns in his main battery, still had six or seven of the 9-pounders in service and all five of the smaller guns on the open deck. The *Richard* had perhaps a dozen cannon still working, including the three topside nines. Each ship had some forty men in the fighting tops of her three masts, and spread behind the bulwarks, shooting from whatever cover they could find, were dozens more. In the total of over five hundred fighting men aboard both vessels, every hand was wielding or serving a weapon.

In that first hour, especially, the battle frequently crescendoed into a nerve-shattering nightmare of lurid light and deafening sound. It was a widening maelstrom of terror, unlike anything anyone aboard had ever known, sucking minds and hearts down into an ever deepening, narrowing vortex of suppressed fear and growing frenzy.

There was the incessant crackle and blast of musketry and swivel guns from the tops; grenades and firebombs rolling on the decks to burst in sharp, spraying flashes; the resounding concussion of the eighteens, joined or interrupted by the steady crashing of the smaller cannon; the clamor of orders bawled by the sweating gunners belowdecks as they exhorted the scurrying powder monkeys to hurry, or urged the gun crews to speed up the swabbing, the loading, the priming, the firing. There was the relentless scourge of shot hammering against and through the hull, decks, bulkheads, masts, sending masses of rended wood and ugly splinters exploding into the air, to crash down finally on some unlucky seaman. Flames, set off by grenades, by loose powder, by the burning wads spewed out with the shot, blazed up in the wreck-strewn interiors as well as on the decks, bringing a stream of hard-breathing men with buckets and tubs of water. Screams of pain and mortal fright arose from the wounded. Defiant shouts and curses broke from the straining throats of fighting men who had become so overwrought that nothing mattered but to kill and smash and kill again. And over all there was the biting, throat-blocking, sulphurous pall of churning smoke that filled the lungs and made eyes stream with tears, sometimes curtaining one man from another only a dozen feet away.

There was even, in those first few moments after the grapple, a spontaneous attempt to board from both ships. Without orders, carried away by the noise and excitement, half a dozen English seamen, wielding pikes and cutlasses, clambered across to the *Richard,* only to be met by twice as many Americans.

The brief, savage scuffle ended with two or three of the boarders crumpled in blood on the deck, and the others retreating. Equally carried away, a few of the *Richard*'s men went in headlong pursuit, actually gaining the enemy deck. They were met by a party of men under Lt. Wright and were rapidly cut down or routed.

As yet, Captain Jones had given no order to board. Wary of committing himself too soon, taking no chance that his first attempt might miscarry, he had decided to hold back until his own topmen had cleared both the foe's tops and open main deck, and silenced its quarterdeck guns. That necessary task he fervently hoped would not require too much time, for he was uncertain just how long he could continue to stand up under the massive pounding of the *Serapis*'s main battery.

Firing at point-blank range—no more than a foot or two for most of the guns—with every discharge the Englishman's eighteens tore away large chunks of the *Richard*'s side and mowed down men. The two ships did not sit stationary in the water under this ferocious cannonading. Often they rolled and shuddered violently with the recoil of the guns, rocking apart for three or four feet, and putting intense strain on the grappling lines and the anchor ropes. Then they would come snugly together again, sides and gun muzzles bumping. There was one unique circumstance connected with this stage of the battle which by itself makes vivid the astonishing conditions in which the gun crews worked, and the extraordinary heroism they displayed in facing death so chillingly near at hand. In order to position the long-handled sponges and rammers for insertion into the gun mouths, it was necessary first to pass the other end of the nine-foot handle out through the gunport. When the two ships were touching, it frequently happened that the outer tip of a handle would actually, if momentarily, pass in through one of the enemy gunports opposite.

Some of the English cannon, with barrels slightly elevated, were taking dead aim at the *Richard*'s gunports. Others, with barrels depressed, were throwing shot into her bottom. A few of the Americans, nerves snapping under the strain of staring straight into smoking muzzles, broke and fled to shelter in the chains forward, where Lt. Dale periodically followed and drove them out. As the minutes passed, though the American cannon continued to reply, the superiority of the English gunners made itself increasingly felt. One by one, the *Richard*'s 12-pounders were being silenced, as carriages were smashed or overturned and barrels dismounted.

On his quarterdeck, Jones felt a hail of grape-shot whistle past. Turning, he saw the flagstaff with its huge American ensign blasted from its perch. It disappeared over the stern, dragging the colors into the water. Two or three of the quarterdeck gunners had also gone down in the same deadly storm, among them Matthew Mease, who now lay prostrate, his hands clutching his bloody head. Jones, bending over him, saw that though stunned he was still conscious.

He detailed a man to assist the badly wounded officer down to the cockpit.

With Mease's departure, the nines were left without an officer. All the midshipmen had been sent to fill in at other stations and there was no one else available at the moment on the quarterdeck. Almost as if he welcomed an excuse to take a direct hand in the fighting, Jones hurried to fill Mease's place, briskly calling out his commands. Before long, he decided to augment his little battery, and with several men assisting him he crossed the deck and unlashed one of the idle portside nines. Pushing, tugging and hauling on ropes, he and his men slowly dragged the 3000-pound cannon to an unused gunport on the starboard side and hooked up the tackle.

When the new gun was in place, Jones trained it on the *Serapis*'s mainmast—painted a bright yellow, it offered a vivid if narrow target. Though it was distant only some seventy feet from Jones's position on the quarterdeck, to bear on it the gun had to be deflected left about forty-five degrees. This made a very awkward angle from which to serve, aim and fire, yet with every second or third shot the hurtling iron went home, hitting the mast at a point some fifteen feet above the deck and gouging away more and more of the three-foot-thick cylinder. The *Serapis,* if by some lucky stroke she did wriggle free, would not get far without a mainmast. And if Jones could succeed soon in bringing it down, the loss might well prompt the British captain to consider surrender.

Even in the heat of battle, Jones had been able to keep the positions of the other ships in his mind. The *Alliance*, he knew, was hove-to about a mile off his stern, and along with everyone else on the *Richard*, he was infuriated by Landais's shameful dawdling. The Frenchman's failure to commit his ship, with its fresh 215-man crew and its eighteen-gun broadside, verged on dereliction of duty. It was with no little sense of relief that Jones now saw that the *Alliance* had begun to move.

Judging by his course, Jones estimated, Landais apparently intended to come up on the Englishman's free side. That approach would require him to sail in a wide semicircle around the two ships, to the north, a time-consuming maneuver. However, once Landais was in place they would have the *Serapis* pinned between them. Then, if cannonading should not prove sufficient, boarding parties could be sent overwhelmingly from both sides. No one aboard the *Richard*, Jones least of all, was prepared for what happened next.

As the *Alliance*, moving at a deliberate pace, crossed from left to right, some hundred yards to the north of the two locked ships, a row of bright red flashes suddenly blossomed along her darkened hull. Jones was appalled. A simultaneous raking broadside, fired at that short distance, was nothing less than insanity. The combined width of the two embattled vessels was hardly seventy-five feet. The shot from the *Alliance* would certainly hit both, doing as much damage to friend as to foe.

A split second later a heavy shower of spreading grapeshot sliced through the *Richard's* bow, cutting down several men on the forecastle. One of these, Master's Mate Joshua Carswell, while being carried to the cockpit repeated over and over, incredulously, that he had been hit by American guns. A little later, as Carswell lay with the other wounded on a piece of blood-soaked canvas awaiting treatment by the harried Dr. Brooke, he died.

It was a blunder on Landais's part that would have been unforgivable even in a midshipman, and in his own mind the enraged Jones branded the French captain as a coward. He had opened fire from a position that was entirely safe from the *Serapis's* idle port battery, and at a distance well beyond the effective range of muskets.

With the *Alliance* moving on, Jones called for his night recognition signals to be displayed—three large lanterns holding thick candles of special wax, hung on a line about thirty feet above the deck, on the forecastle, in the waist and at the mizzenmast. Because of the smoke and the flames, he knew, these signals might not always be visible, yet something had to be done to warn Landais off. The *Alliance,* however, instead of rounding-to on the *Serapis,* again surprised everyone by veering north, away from the battle. As it receded into the night, its dark shape was followed by dozens of pairs of puzzled eyes, all widening in disbelief.

There was no leisure, just then, for Jones to worry further about the mad behavior of Landais.

From below, two reports reached him which indicated that, for the *Richard,* the situation had become critical.

Lt. Dale, drenched in sweat and looking exhausted, appeared on the quarterdeck to announce that the entire main battery had been silenced. Every one of the fourteen starboard twelves had been disabled or dismounted. Casualties, moreover, had been high, with about half of the gun crews wounded or dead.

The second report came from the chief carpenter, John Gunnison, who since the start of the battle had made periodic reports to Jones on the condition of the ship's bottom. Despite unflagging efforts to plug the holes, and the constant working of four pumps, the numerous leaks were steadily gaining. The water already in the hold had reached a depth of more than four feet. Another three or four feet and the vessel would be in danger of sinking, at least might heel over or settle by bow or stern. Also, Gunnison went on, there were the hundred or so English prisoners to consider. Some had already been wounded or killed, and the remainder, because of the relentless fire of the enemy and the rising water, were close to panic. They were demanding to be taken higher or released.

Jones, careful to conceal his anxiety, ordered that the prisoners be left where they were until further notice. Then he directed Dale to take charge of the pumps and to keep them working at maximum capacity. Also, Dale was to round up as many men with muskets as he could spare from other posts and set them to guard the lower gunports. Jones did not want English boarders stealing into the *Richard* belowdecks.

As Dale and Gunnison departed, Jones sank wearily onto a piece of timber, seeking a moment's respite in which to make a cooler assessment of his gloomy prospects. As he sat, a young sailor rushed over from one of the 9-pounders, his eyes wide with fear and excitement. "For God's sake, Captain," he cried distractedly, "why don't you strike!"

Jones peered at the wavering young sailor, then slowly rose. The man must have heard the two reports, he guessed, and had concluded from them that the *Richard* was beaten, that there remained not even the glimmer of a hope for victory. "I will sink first," replied Jones evenly as he turned back to his guns, "I will never strike."

Had he waited too long to send his boarders away, he wondered. Yet it was still impossible to tell whether the enemy's main deck had been cleared enough to assure control by boarders, especially in a night assault. Fighting hand-to-hand in the darkness, the Americans would be at a disadvantage, might easily find themselves slaying each other rather than Englishmen. Further, the enemy captain almost certainly would have a large force concealed just below, ready to swarm up at the first hint of an attack. In any event, with the *Richard*'s main battery gone, leaving her with only the three nines on the quarterdeck, and with his men falling victim to every boom of the *Serapis*'s cannon, if a boarding was to be attempted at all it could not be delayed much longer.

The enemy's tops seemed to Jones to have been cleared, at least the firing from the platforms on all three masts had ceased. In fact, however, there was still one English sailor staunchly holding out in the *Serapis*'s foretop, and it was Lt. Stack's men in the *Richard*'s maintop who finally brought him down.

The distance between the two platforms was about fifty feet. Since the ships were bow to stern, the masts were not directly opposite each other, and the English foretop in addition was wrapped in shadows only flickeringly illuminated by the flames below. Firing from behind the mast, this lone British seaman had picked off several of the men in the *Richard*'s fore- and maintops before he was discovered. As soon as Lt. Stack spotted this "skulking tar" he ordered several of the men around him to reserve their fire, with muskets leveled. When the man again half-showed himself, preparing to shoot, Stack snapped an order. The muskets blazed, there was a cry, and a dark shape plummeted through the smoke to the *Serapis*'s forecastle deck.

This alert action, as it turned out, was of greater importance than anyone realized, for it paved the way for a daring exploit by one of the American seamen, an exploit whose unforeseeable results would radically alter the tide of battle.

With the English tops now apparently cleared, one of Lt. Stack's men, a Scot named William Hamilton, volunteered to take a bucket of grenades and crawl out along the main yardarm, the tip of which hung over the enemy nearly amidships. From there, Hamilton suggested, he could lob grenades practically straight down, wherever they would do the most damage. Stack agreed, and Hamilton, clutching the heavy bucket in one hand, and with a smoldering slow match clamped between his teeth, inched his way along the yardarm on his stomach, his presence hidden from watchers below by the folds of the clewed-up mainsail just underneath.

At the yardarm's end, Hamilton began lighting and dropping the grenades, wherever the drifting shadows indicated there might be a group of men. Soon his searching eye was caught by a large hatch in the *Serapis*'s waist, some fifteen feet to the left of his precarious perch. The cover had been disturbed and was lying askew, leaving a corner of the hatchway open to the skies.

Carefully, Hamilton swung his arm once or twice, gauging the distance, then released a grenade. It missed the opening and exploded on the deck. Lighting another, he tried again. This time the sputtering missile bounced off the combing of the hatch, then fell straight down through the narrow slit and into the darkness below.

Captain Pearson could hardly believe his good fortune. He had now been under fire for more than two hours, had inflicted severe punishment on his foe, and still the rest of Jones's squadron had shown no inclination to join in. The single broadside, delivered from a distance by the wandering frigate some ten minutes before, had hit both ships, had in fact done little damage to the *Serapis*. And, according to reports, Jones's main battery had been completely destroyed, while the *Serapis* was still working nine of her heavy guns, methodically tearing apart the enemy's hull and bottom.

Against that, the Americans had managed to silence his tops, and had practically cleared the main deck, undoubtedly as a prelude to boarding. But any such attempt, Pearson felt confident, would be quickly repulsed by the force he had in reserve just below. In reality, his greatest threat at the moment was neither an American boarding party nor shot, but fire. Half a dozen times in different parts of the ship flames had started up, and had grown and spread so rapidly and fiercely that it had been only with the greatest exertion that the men were able to control or extinguish them. The most significant question now was how much longer could Jones continue to stand up under the pounding of the eighteens? By rights, according to everything Pearson had learned during his three decades at sea, the pirate should have struck long ago.

Two hours was a very long time for men, even the hardy, well-trained sailors of the *Serapis,* to be handling guns uninterruptedly, and at such incredibly close quarters. The drain on the nerves even by itself had caused numbers of the crew to break and run for cover. Yet it was critical that the fire of the eighteens should go on briskly, and if possible be increased. Nine guns firing at will could provide an almost continuous barrage, the very noise of which, at this stage of the battle, could be almost as important, in its demoralizing effects on the enemy, as the shot.

To urge his men to greater effort, Pearson sent Sailing Master William Wheatley below to deliver a message of encouragement to Lt. Stanhope: The enemy appeared close to surrender—there must be no flagging of spirit—double-shot all the guns—select targets carefully—remain cool and aim without haste—a glorious victory was theirs this day. Stanhope assured Wheately that his men, though they had taken severe casualties, were still showing great spirit and had already begun to savor the triumph.

It was only a few minutes after Wheatley's departure that the grenade thrown by seaman Hamilton came bouncing onto the lower gun deck, its presence unnoticed, the noise of its descent lost in the general uproar. It rolled to rest, its fuse nearly consumed, beside several powder cartridges just behind gun number six. A second later a tremendous roar shook the whole interior of the lower gun deck, from the mainmast aft.

In reality, it was not a single explosion, but a rapid series of two or three smaller blasts, leaping along the straggling line of extra cartridges, and end-ing in a single, deep-echoing crash of thunder. Almost on the instant, an impenetrable pall of thick, dark-gray smoke boiled all along the deck, veiling the carnage among the gun crews. Those who were not killed outright, or badly wounded, groped about in a stupor. Unaware of the reason for the catastrophe, they imagined that the ship's powder magazine itself had been hit and that the whole ship was about to go up.

Half a dozen frenzied men clawed their way to the aftermost gunport, where the space between the ships widened. They scrambled through and jumped out into the darkness, hitting the water almost on top of one another. Paddling on the surface, they all peered up apprehensively at the shadowy bulk of the ship's stern. Though smoke continued to roll out of the gunports, the minutes passed and there were no further explosions.

One of those who jumped was sailmaker Robert Ozard, who had been filling in at the guns and who had been lucky enough to escape the holocaust with no more than burned hands. Anxious to get back aboard, he seized a line that was trailing over the side and pulled himself up, painful hand over painful hand, his feet pressing against the ship. Exhausted, he was hauling himself over the quarterdeck railing when he looked up and found himself staring into the barrel of a musket, leveled by a marine. "Oh, Lord," he cried, and in his fright could say no more. Captain Pearson, standing nearby, recognized the man and called quickly, "Don't kill him, he's one of our people!" Ozard thanked the captain and received permission to go below for treatment of his hands.

In the noisy cockpit, crowded with at least fifty wounded and with Surgeon Bannatyne and his assistants working feverishly, Ozard stopped one of the hurrying assistants and asked if there were any rubbing oil for his hands. There was no more oil to be had, he was told as the assistant moved abruptly away. Ozard looked round at the prostrate men, all suffering from wounds far worse than his; then with a shrug he turned and left. Climbing to the gun deck, he found the smoke still seething and his old station in a shambles. He walked forward and joined the crew of one of the eighteens that was still firing, his burns all but forgotten.

Lt. Stanhope, his face and both of his hands badly scorched, had also plunged overboard through the aftermost gunport. For some minutes he continued splashing between the ships, losing his shoes in the process. Then he swam around to the stern where he was safe from sharpshooters, and climbed back aboard. He descended to the cockpit, found there was no oil, from somewhere turned up a tub of hog's lard and had it smeared on his tender skin. Slipping into the nearby cabin of purser Malcolm Cockburne, he wrung out his heavy uniform coat and borrowed a pair of shoes. Downing a hasty glass of wine, he returned above to inspect the damage.

About forty men, he found, had been put out of action. Half of them were dead, and of the twenty or so wounded it was plain that some of them would not live long. As for the guns, five of the eighteens had been lost, all those from the mainmast aft. Carriages were overturned or smashed to splinters, the guns themselves strewn about as if they were toys. Weighing some two tons apiece, they were impossible to remount, even if the carriages could have been salvaged. That left the *Serapis* with only four heavy cannon, all of them forward.

It was the presence of extra cartridges on deck, Stanhope concluded, that had caused the disaster. Regulations forbade any accumulation of powder, precisely to avoid such accidents, but in the confusion of battle it sometimes happened. Despite the denials of chief gunner James Shaine—"no more but what was needed," was his reply to the question whether extra powder had been lying on the deck— Stanhope was satisfied that a simple breech of rules had been responsible. The powder monkeys had brought cartridges up from the magazine faster than they could be used, and had left them lying in a tight row behind the guns. Just how they had been set off, Stanhope could not decide—perhaps something flammable or a grenade thrown across from gunport to gunport.

Captain Pearson, pacing his quarterdeck, was stunned by the sudden worsening of his position. He knew that, aside from the loss of men and firepower, such a devastating setback, happening so unexpectedly, was often accompanied by a plunge in morale among the survivors, taking the heart out of them and draining their will to continue. For the first time since the battle began, Pearson was face to face with the likelihood that in fighting on, he might only be fruitlessly increasing his casualties. With his main battery now halved, whenever one of the frigates decided to come down on him, his only humane response would be surrender.

Pearson turned to look out over his stern, searching for the other enemy ships. Through the drifting smoke he caught sight of the *Countess,* far to the north, lying quietly alongside one of the frigates. That battle, at any rate, was over.

The moon, after shining so brightly at first, now disappeared behind a bank of clouds and Pearson had to cast his eye back and forth in the dark before he could locate the other American frigate. He spotted it about a mile to the northeast, moving slowly on the port tack under topsails only. If she held that course, Pearson concluded ruefully, she would be alongside the *Serapis* in less than ten minutes.

Aboard the *Richard,* abovedecks and below, fore and aft, fire had now become as much of a threat as the English guns. Crackling suddenly to life, often simultaneously in two or three locations, feeding especially on the splintered pitch-soaked wreckage that now lay tumbled everywhere, flames repeatedly flared up, the iridescent reds and yellows weirdly illuminating the abysmal darkness of the lower decks.

Throughout the ship, parties of sweating men were kept busy hauling water in tubs, buckets, jugs, anything that was handy. Several times on the orlop deck smoldering flames crept to within a few feet of the magazine before being detected. At one point, fire even swept up the tar-encrusted rigging of the mainmast, setting ablaze not only the topsails but the fighting platform itself. The men stationed there experienced some anxious moments in their efforts to subdue the flames that were eating away at their support. "The water which we had in a tub in the forepart of the top," Midshipman Fanning recalled, "was expended without extinguishing the fire. We next had recourse to our clothes, by pulling off our coats and jackets and throwing them upon the fire, and stamping upon them." The fire was eventually smothered.

Almost equally threatening was the condition of the ship's hull, now battered to the point where it seemed miraculous that she was still afloat, still riding on an even keel. "A person must have been an eyewitness," Jones said afterward, "to form a just idea of the tremendous scene of carnage, wreck and ruin that everywhere appeared."

Nearly the whole starboard side, from about the mainmast aft and from the waterline to the gunwale, had been demolished, leaving the interiors of the two gun decks exposed. The shot from the

Serapis, carrying across the ship, had also beaten out much of the opposite side, so that the shot thrown by her remaining eighteens were now being wasted as they sped in at one side and out through the other, touching nothing and splashing into the water hundreds of yards beyond. The stern had also been smashed to pieces, with almost the entire transom shot away and the counters driven in. Many of the heavy support timbers, especially those on which depended the lower gun deck, had been cracked and both the poop and the quarterdeck now sagged alarmingly, appearing in immediate danger of collapse. The huge rudder, askew and hanging by a single pintle, was also ready to drop off.

In the forward part of the ship, because the *Serapis*'s after guns had been silenced, the *Richard* exhibited less damage; and it was here, in the waist and on the forecastle, that Jones was now hurrying back and forth in a feverish effort to prepare his boarders. Mustering men from the deck and calling them up from below, he armed them with any weapons available and stationed them under cover along the bulwarks. At a signal, led by Jones himself, they would rise as one, rush in a line over the *Richard*'s side, and try to sweep the enemy's main deck. They would then fight their way down through the ship, deck by deck, until the last Englishman had surrendered and the last gun fell silent. Now, crouching out of sight, some fifty men, most on the forecastle, awaited Jones's command for what they nervously prayed would be the final, decisive action of the three-hour battle.

A loud exclamation from a nearby seaman brought Jones's head erect, his eyes searching past the *Serapis* and into the night beyond. The *Alliance,* sailing at a leisurely pace on the port tack, was again approaching, this time with her mainsails clewed up as if prepared to enter the fight. "I now thought the battle at an end," wrote Jones later, recalling that moment of welcome relief. The boarding attempt, he decided, would have to be delayed. He could not risk exposing his men on the enemy's deck if the *Alliance,* instead of grappling, should open fire with her cannon on the *Serapis*'s free side. In any case, if only Landais this time played his part properly, there might be no need to run the hazard of boarding.

Moving slowly under its topsails, its path a wide semicircle that kept it well away from the Englishman's portside guns, the *Alliance* curved south around the two ships, closing to within about fifty yards as it glided past the locked bow and stern. Then, to the shocked surprise of the watching Americans her guns boomed out raggedly and a hail of grapeshot and bar shot rained on both ships. As she passed on, bringing the *Richard* more and more between herself and the *Serapis,* several of the guns that had not joined in the first broadside now fired. The shot this time hit only the *Richard,* smashing into her port quarter just abaft the beam. As the echoes died away, a score of bellowing voices arose from the *Richard* all shouting angrily that the damn Frenchman was firing on the wrong ship, and cursing Landais as a coward, a traitor, a madman.

On the maintop platform, Lt. Stack pleaded at the top of his voice, "I beg you will not sink us!" while half a dozen of his marksmen, spitting oaths and imprecations, aimed their muskets down on the decks of the receding *Alliance*. Only Stack's hurried threats kept them from firing.

Captain Jones, in "utter astonishment" at this repetition of the original blunder, now added his own voice to the general cry, roaring across the water for the *Alliance* to cease firing and to "lay the enemy on board!" But that ship was already out of hearing. Its curving progress had carried it swiftly away from the *Richard*'s off side until it was separated from the combatants by several hundred yards. Those watching thought at first it was hauling off, deserting the fight as it had done before. But then it picked up speed, circling north as the wind came over its stern.

Jones, anticipating that Landais would next cross his bow, sent Midshipmen Linthwaite and Coram rushing to the forecastle with speaking trumpets. As the *Alliance*, a few minutes later, began bearing down, both officers shouted that Captain Jones's orders were to cease firing and to go alongside the enemy, prepared for boarding. Coram requested confirmation that the orders had been heard and understood, and he thought he heard a faint "aye, aye" float back in answer. But as the dark shadow of the frigate swept past from left to right, her broadside once again thundered out, the shot slicing as before into both ships.

In the maintop, his patience evaporated, Lt. Stack made no effort this time to restrain his angry men. Instead he actually shouted for them to open fire on the *Alliance*. A dozen muskets leaped to shoulders and were cocked, but the offender had moved on and was soon screened from the maintop platform by the *Richard*'s topsails, leaving Stack's sharpshooters growling in frustration.

His temper seething, now almost convinced that Landais's wild assault could only have been a deliberate attack on the *Richard*—though for what reason he could not conceive—Jones hurried forward to check on the damage done to the boarding party. He was appalled by the scene that met him. Lying on the forecastle deck were some ten or a dozen men, half of them dead. All were victims of the *Alliance,* he was sure, since the *Serapis* had no guns bearing forward and all of her tops had been cleared. The survivors on the forecastle had hastily scrambled for cover, leaping and diving over and under obstacles in their race to escape the rain of death from the frigate. As a result the boarding party had melted away and was now scattered throughout the ship.

Jones ordered the wounded taken below; then he told Linthwaite and Coram to form up the boarders once more. There was no more time to waste, he said, and the *Alliance* must now be considered an enemy, whether deliberate or not. Before Landais came on the scene again, the *Serapis* must be taken.

As Jones turned to leave the forecastle he was stopped by several of the ship's officers, in company with one of the marine lieutenants. The situation was hopeless, urged the lieutenant. Wouldn't the captain consider striking? Why sacrifice more men? Halting only long enough to throw a pained look at the lieutenant and the others with him, Jones turned away in silence. Though he respected these men, and though up to now they had fought well, it saddened him to see how they were ready to accept defeat just at the moment—the very moment!—when the greatest glory awaited them. A victory now, under these deplorable circumstances, would make their names immortal, would send the fame of the scorned American navy ringing around the world. Didn't they understand that?

While the *Alliance* had been creating havoc on the main deck, another drama, one of even more threatening proportions, had been rapidly developing below.

The chief carpenter, John Gunnison, after his latest inspection of the hold, had reported anxiously to Lt. Dale on the lower gun deck that the water stood at a depth of nearly seven feet. It was still rising and the English prisoners, convinced that the ship was about to sink, were riotously demanding their release. Dale had left the gun deck to carry Gunnison's report to Jones, and he had reached the quarterdeck just about the time the *Alliance* had made her second pass, crossing the *Richard*'s bow.

Within minutes, a dismaying rumor sped among the men belowdecks. Both Jones and Dale had been hit, it was said, and were either dead or dying. When the rumor reached the fretting Gunnison it had expanded to include several other officers, and it struck Gunnison with all the weight of dreadful truth. He quickly realized that with the second and third lieutenants absent from the ship, no one remained who was qualified to command, not the three Irishmen, certainly none of the young midshipmen. In such a rare situation, he concluded, it was up to the highest ranking petty officers to take charge.

Gunnison now sought out the ship's master at arms, John Burbank, and the chief gunner, Henry Gardner, and assured them that the ship was on the brink of going down. The prisoners must be released, he insisted, so they might save themselves. According to regulations, the care of prisoners fell within the duties of the master at arms, and Burbank now agreed that for humanity's sake they must be let go. That meant that the *Richard* must surrender, for it was inconceivable that she could continue the battle with over a hundred of the enemy freely roaming her decks. Henry Gardner agreed, urging that in any case the time had come to strike the colors. With Jones and Dale dead or out of action, and no officers left above the rank of midshipman or sublieutenant, it became his duty as chief gunner to make that decision. While the master at arms started down to the hold, the other two hurried to the quarterdeck.

On the forecastle, after leaving the marine lieutenant, Jones was walking back to his station with the 9-pounders. Suddenly he became aware of running men, saw others climbing hurriedly out of the hatchways or milling aimlessly on deck, glimpsed a few even leaping overboard. Instantly he guessed what had happened; the prisoners had either broken free or been released, and there was now a horde of angry Englishmen running loose on his crippled ship. Before he could take any action, however, he was amazed to hear, from the direction of the poop deck, a clamor of voices bawling, "Quarter! Quarter! For god's sake, quarter!" Someone on the *Richard* was frantically offering to surrender!

"What damned rascals are they!" Jones shouted as he raced aft. "Shoot them! Kill them!" He pulled a pistol from his belt as he ran, forgetting that he had earlier emptied the weapon at the *Serapis,* and had not yet reloaded it. Bounding up the ladder unto the poop deck he spotted the gunner, Henry Gardner, waving a lantern over the side and begging at the top of his lungs for "Quarter!" Beside him, also bellowing his willingness to surrender, stood the carpenter, Gunnison.

Happening to look around, Gunnison was shocked to see the captain he thought dead or disabled striding across the poop deck not twenty feet away, his eyes alight, his face a thundercloud. In a sudden panic at the realization that his actions might

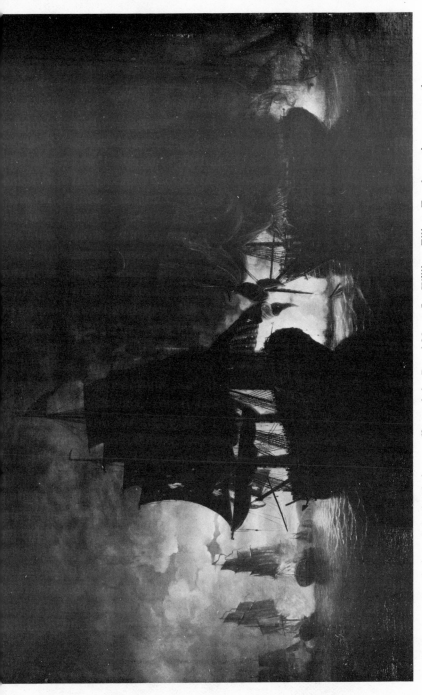

Contemporary oil painting of the battle by an officer of the Royal Navy, Lt. William Elliott. For dramatic purposes the artist has telescoped several different moments of the battle. (*Courtesy U.S. Naval Academy*)

As the two ships grappled, both sides made brief, spontaneous attempts to board. Here the Americans gain the deck of the *Serapis* only to be repulsed. Drawing by J. Davidson, 1877. (*Courtesy New York Public Library*)

Approximate positions of the two ships just after the grappling. The
Bonhomme Richard is on the left. Drawing by J. Davidson, 1877.
(*Courtesy New York Public Library*)

About a half hour before the end of the battle the American frigate
Alliance fired on the embattled ships, hitting both friend and
foe. With his ship sinking, his main battery silenced, some of his
men crying for quarter, this was the low point of Jones's fortunes.

Engraving by J. Boydell from a contemporary oil painting by
Richard Paton.
(*Courtesy U.S. Naval Academy*)

Just before the battle's end, Captain Pearson sent his boarders
swarming into the firelit darkness of the American's decks. Minutes
later the Englishmen were thrown back to their own ship.
Contemporary engraving by Chappel.
(*Culver*)

be construed as cowardice, even outright treachery, stopping neither to think nor explain, Gunnison broke from the railing and scampered down the ladder to the quarterdeck, running to hide himself from his captain's anger. In Jones's eyes, the carpenter's flight provided instant proof that the two trusted petty officers, for whatever cause, had turned traitor and had tried to usurp his authority.

Ignoring Gunnison, Jones with great deliberation leveled his pistol at Gardner and pulled the trigger. There was only a click. Gardner turned, saw Jones brandishing the firearm, and he too made a dash for the ladder. Grasping the pistol by its barrel, Jones flung the weapon with all his strength at the fleeing gunner. It flew straight for Gardner's head and crunched dully against the back of his skull just as he reached the top of the ladder. Gardner collapsed, his momentum carrying him over the deck's edge. Slithering heavily down the narrow steps, he sprawled on the deck below and lay still.

His fury still shaking him, Jones stood alone on the poop deck. Below, by the fitful light of several fires that were burning unchecked along the bulwarks, he could see many of the English prisoners standing in confused bunches or stumbling over wreckage, his own men running among them with muskets at the ready. Then a voice, faint but clear, arose from the *Serapis*. It was Captain Pearson, speaking through a trumpet from his quarterdeck. "Sir, do you ask for quarter," Pearson was calling anxiously, "do you ask for quarter?"

Jones strode to the railing of the poop deck, where he could look down the entire length of the enemy vessel. Dim in the shadows he could just make out the form of the English captain, not fifty feet away, holding the trumpet. "No, sir," he replied loudly, "I do not ask for quarter."

He paused, his tired brain searching for words that would wipe out the distasteful memory of his subordinate's defection, some defiant words that might be hurled as if from a cannon. Raising his head high, he shouted so that every syllable would hit home: "I—have—not—yet—*begun*—to—fight!"

Descending to the quarterdeck, Jones detailed some men to carry the unconscious Gardner below. His most urgent task now was to round up and establish control over the roaming prisoners, before they had a chance to realize their opportunity and begin to act in concert. But Lt. Dale, as it turned out, had this potentially explosive situation already well in hand.

Reporting to Jones, Dale explained that he had set the greater part of the prisoners to manning the pumps under guard, thus releasing the *Richard*'s own men to rejoin the fight. It had not been difficult to convince them, disorganized as they were, that the ship could only be kept above the water by a violent application of the pumps—they had seen the frightening depth of water in the hold with their own eyes. Dale had also sealed off the powder magazine from any attempt at tampering, stationing extra guards around it and in the passageways.

Satisfied, Jones turned back to the 9-pounder he had been serving. As he approached, he was surprised and greatly heartened to see that the badly wounded Matthew Mease had returned to his post, and was vigorously directing the fire of the little battery, his head swathed in bloody bandages.

Captain Pearson stood his dimly lit quarter-deck almost alone, beset by wracking doubts. All his training, his instincts, told him that it was useless to continue the battle, that the time had come for him to surrender his ship.

The enemy commander, it appeared, was a man of unyielding will, almost inhuman, who seemed ready to send every living soul aboard both ships to the bottom rather than accept defeat. But for Pearson to push the fight to that awful extremity, in his own anguished view, would be an utterly savage waste of life. He was now, he judged, in a position that left him, whatever happened, without the slightest hope of victory. Even if Jones, by some twist of fate, should be brought to strike his colors, it would be no real triumph for the *Serapis;* at least it would be a woefully short-lived one. There would still be the two remaining frigates to deal with. If only one of the two should engage, then the *Serapis,* severely damaged in her upper parts and bereft of the greater part of her armament, must soon haul down her flag.

Yet there did exist a last chance, even if a slim one, for salvation, and it was that single forlorn hope that now made Pearson hesitate. If the American were to strike, or if the *Serapis* could somehow be wrenched loose from that fanatic death grip, she might be able to make a run for the friendly shore. There could no longer be any need, Pearson felt sure, to continue the fight as a delaying action. The entire convoy must long since have reached safety. Yet doubts persisted: Could he, in good conscience, in all humanity, prolong the bloodshed just on the tenuous hope of escaping?

Pearson's dilemma was solved for him, and in an unexpected way. Dramatically, there appeared on the *Serapis*'s quarterdeck one of the English prisoners from the *Richard,* a certain Captain Johnston (first name unknown). Master of the brig *Union,* captured by Jones a few days before, Johnston had been among those prisoners set to work on the pumps. With cool presence of mind, he had awaited an opportunity to slip away unnoticed, then had crawled out through an unattended gunport on the lower deck, expecting at any moment to receive a musket ball in the back. Jumping easily across to one of the *Serapis*'s gunports, he identified himself to the wary English sailors and asked to speak to the captain. Escorted hurriedly to Pearson, he gave a full report on the critical state of the American ship, told of the large force of English prisoners loose on the decks, described the hold full of water. It was only a matter of a very short time, he insisted, until Jones must strike or sink.

His hopes of escape suddenly soaring, perhaps envisioning a return to England with Captain Jones himself a captive, Pearson sent a message below to Lt. Stanhope: At all costs the fire of the eighteens must be increased, and the guns should be depressed to throw the shot into the enemy's bottom.

Ten minutes passed without a change in the situation on either side, then twenty. The only sounds disturbing the quiet of the night were the booming of the four English cannon, the sharp reply of Mease's three 9-pounders, the frequent blast of musket or grenade, the pervasive hiss of fires, and the mournful cries of the wounded abovedecks and below. The American captain, it very much appeared, had meant what he said.

One last chance remained, but it was with reluctance that Pearson employed it. He would risk a boarding, he decided, though in the enveloping blackness, with men slashing blindly at each other, there could be little chance of a clear-cut decision.

Some minutes later Lt. Wright had formed up a party of about thirty men and had lined them along the bulwarks wherever the flames parted. The signal was piped, and the men swarmed up waving pikes and cutlasses, looking like demons in the lurid half-light. Somehow they scrambled in a line across to the *Richard*'s side, leaping headlong into the gloom of the main deck—and there they were met by a disciplined force of double their number, pouncing swiftly out of the shadows. Disorganized, demoralized by their inability to identify targets, the Englishmen within a few minutes turned and fled, jumping from ship to ship in frantic haste, some missing their footing and falling with terrified cries into the black depths between the ships.

Even as his boarders stumbled back in retreat, Pearson knew that the end had come. The *Serapis*'s mainmast, which for an hour had been under the remarkably accurate fire of the *Richard*'s quarter-deck guns, had finally cracked. Its trembling, 140-foot length had now begun to tilt to port, away from the foe. It remained upright only by virtue of the numerous braces and preventer stays, and because its yardarms were still entangled with those of the *Richard*. It could not retain its position much longer, and when it went it would take with it a part of the mizzenmast. Though Pearson still might get his ship loose and into the open water, with only a weakened foremast holding a ragged sail, there was little hope of reaching shore.

Having made his decision, Pearson wasted no further time. Stepping up to the railing, he lifted his trumpet and shouted: "Sir, I have struck! I ask for quarter!"

Captain Jones heard the call almost without emotion. Glancing at the *Serapis*'s stern, he saw that her flag was still flying, in the absence of wind hanging nearly limp. "If you have struck," he shouted, "haul down your ensign."

Pearson walked aft, took hold of the fluttering lower edges of the huge flag, then ripped it nail by nail from its staff. Gathering in its voluminous folds, he gave it into the care of a nearby seaman.

"Cease firing!" Jones called briskly to those around him on the quarterdeck. "She has struck! Send word below."

As quiet gradually settled over the *Richard,* only a few men able to muster the energy for a cheer, Lt. Dale hurried up and asked Jones's permission to board. The English captain should be taken off as soon as possible, he urged. The permission was hesitantly given, and only at Dale's enthusiastic pleading. There had not been a sufficient interval, Jones felt, for word of the surrender to have reached throughout the defeated ship, or for the fighting blood of her men to have calmed. A too hasty approach during the transition could be dangerous since isolated groups of men, spirits still inflamed, might wish to continue the battle.

Not waiting to discuss the point, with sword in hand Dale called Midshipman Mayrant and a number of others to follow him, then he seized a line that was trailing down from a main yardarm and swung across the gap from railing to railing. Dropping to the deck, he proceeded aft in search of the captain. Mayrant, following close behind, no sooner reached the *Serapis* than he had the misfortune to become the last casualty of the battle. As he set foot on the enemy's deck, a figure stirred in the shadows. There was a glint of thrusting metal, and Mayrant crumpled in pain, his thigh gashed open. The men arriving behind him assisted him back to the *Richard*.

On the *Serapis*'s quarterdeck, Dale walked up to a man he judged to be the commander and introduced himself. "Sir, I have orders," he explained politely, "to send you on board the ship alongside."

Before Pearson could respond, Lt. Wright joined the group, glanced in puzzlement at Dale, then inquired of his captain whether the enemy had struck. Dale interrupted. "No, sir, the contrary," he said, "he has struck to us."

Wright ignored Dale and looked steadily at Pearson, awaiting an answer.

"Yes, I have," replied Pearson, his tone subdued.

"I have nothing more to say," finished Wright, a note of disappointment in his voice, and he turned to leave. Dale called him back, however, explaining that he must transfer to the other ship.

"If you will permit me to go below," Wright suggested, "I will silence the firing of the lower deck guns."

Dale, not caring to leave so high ranking an officer at large, refused. Someone of lesser rank should be sent down, he directed. With that Pearson and Wright were escorted across a plank to the *Richard*'s deck, Dale remaining behind.

In the pale yellow glow of several lanterns the English officers came face to face with Captain Jones, and were introduced. Pearson removed his sword and held it toward his conquerer. "Sir, you have fought like a hero," said Jones as he accepted the token of surrender, "and I make no doubt that your sovereign will reward you." He then returned the sword, saying Pearson was welcome to continue wearing it.

The meeting between the two captains was brief and formal; but before they parted, Pearson to be escorted below, the British officer paused to ask a question. Of what nationality was the *Richard*'s officers and crew mainly composed, he inquired. "Americans," answered Jones.

"Well, then," said Pearson, a touch of relief shading his tired voice, "it has been diamond cut diamond with us."

A sharp, rending noise made everyone look toward the *Serapis*. The mainmast, they saw, had begun to fall. Foot by foot it leaned, like a majestic tree coming down in the forest, snapping lines, pulling the other masts and sails askew, yanking the mizzen topsail from its yardarm. Gathering momentum, its long length finally crashed down against the port bulwark. As the jagged bottom end leaped free of the broken stump, the slender tip, with its small ensign streaming in the breeze, hit the water with a great splash far overboard.

3

The end of the Bonhomme Richard

Victory brought no rest for John Paul Jones and his men. Still to be faced were two immediate hazards, each almost as harrowing and dangerous as the English guns had been. There were the fires, large and small, still burning fiercely, some in locations that were nearly inaccessible, especially on the orlop deck where the powder magazine was threatened. And there was the water in the inundated hold, steadily deepening and appearing already to have passed the critical level. In addition, there existed a third peril, only a little less pressing—the warships of the Royal Navy which, as every man aboard the *Richard* fully anticipated, must even then be racing from bases in the north and south to converge on Flamborough Head.

As fire-fighting parties spread through the ship, Jones detailed other men to assist in the arduous task of repairing the bottom and pumping out the hold. At the same time he sent orders to Lt. Dale on the *Serapis* to cut the two ships loose. The *Richard* would proceed easterly under light sail, he instructed, putting as great a distance as possible between herself and the watching eyes ashore before dawn. Only the wide expanse of the North Sea itself now offered a haven from pursuit, and perhaps, if fate had one last kindness to bestow, the morning would bring a lowering sky and veiling fog. The *Serapis* and the *Countess,* Jones ordered, were to trail behind the *Richard.* All three consorts were asked to stand by.

With the grappling hooks cast off and the big anchor fluke of the English ship wrenched from its tenacious grip, the *Richard* drifted free. On the *Serapis*'s foremast and the stump of the mizzen, sails were set. These Dale ordered all aback, and the helm put over, to swing the ship to port.

Dale had been constantly on his feet, his nerves strung tight, since he had rushed half-dressed on deck some twelve hours before. Now with the battle done, the danger past, he felt the energy draining from him, his muscles going slack, vague pains starting up his legs. As he waited for the ship to come round, he wearily took a seat on the binnacle, and minutes passed before he became aware that the ship was not paying off as she should, in fact was hardly moving. Thinking that the wheel ropes might have been severed, he sent a man below to investigate. The ropes, the man reported, were intact.

Irritated, in a hurry to discover the cause of the delay, Dale jumped down from the binnacle—and went sprawling flat on the deck as his right leg collapsed under him. Gazing down at his leg in astonishment, he saw that the white stocking was ripped and covered with blood, and that the flesh of the calf was gashed open. He must have been hit sometime during the battle, he decided, but in his excitement had not even felt it.

Helped to his feet, Dale resumed his place on the binnacle. As he sat, the wound throbbing, the sailing master of the *Serapis* approached "From your orders, Lieutenant," he said, "I judge you are not aware that we have an anchor down." Dale confessed his ignorance and was about to order the anchor up, when he caught sight of Lt. Henry Lunt standing among the prize party nearby.* With pains now shooting up his leg and a general weakness stealing over him, he delegated command of the *Serapis* to Lt. Lunt, telling him to cut the anchor

* *Just how or when Lt. Lunt boarded the* Serapis *is one of the few points about this battle that remains wholly unknown. For further discussion see Part IV, pp. 111–113, and the Notes, pp. 165–166.*

cable and follow the *Richard*. He was then put into one of the small boats and returned to his own ship to have the wound dressed.

With the fire-fighters tearing out planking, bulkheads and deckheads to get at the smoldering flames, the battle against fire on the *Richard* went on through most of the night. On the orlop deck the curling smoke persisted to such a degree that Jones at last decided that he would take no further risk with the powder. The small casks were passed gingerly along a human chain, up through the hatches, and stacked on the main deck, ready if necessary to be thrown overboard.

At about 5 A.M. the first murky streaks of light began to seep through the darkness over the eastern horizon and within an hour Jones saw happily that his wish had been granted. Heavy clouds hung low in the sky, a light fog rolled along the surface of the water, the haze in every direction reducing visibility to a mile or two. It was a desolate panorama to greet the haggard eyes of those who had passed through the hell of the night before, but to the men of the *Bonhomme Richard* the day could not have been more lovely.

Through the night the men toiling at the leaks had made little progress. Most were complaining openly that the effort was useless, that the ship was doomed. Half agreeing, yet wanting to return to France on his own quarterdeck, to possess the living proof of the extraordinary nature of the battle and of his victory, Jones hoisted distress signals, calling for aid from his consorts. He would bring the *Richard* home even if it meant towing her.

Captain Cottineau responded from the *Pallas* with a party of men including his carpenters. Other parties arrived from the *Vengeance,* and even the *Alliance,* and all were set to work in the hold. By midmorning the last of the fires had been quenched, releasing more men to help in the fight against the water, yet it was all to no avail. Finally, James Bragg, chief carpenter of the *Alliance,* and Captain Cottineau both pronounced the shattered bottom absolutely beyond repair, the ship definitely past saving.

Still Jones clung to a last hope. He gave orders to lighten ship, beginning with the useless 18-pounders, all six of which, he said, must be dumped overboard. By itself, that would get rid of some twelve tons, allowing the ship to rise somewhat, and increasing her snail's pace a little. Tugging and levering the big guns, the weary men shoved them one by one through the gaping holes in the ship's side.

Jones, in the meantime, had himself rowed over to inspect the *Serapis.* If, finally, the *Richard* must be abandoned, he would transfer his command to the English vessel.

On the *Serapis* Jones saw that the enemy had taken severe damage in her upper parts, but surprisingly little below. Her hull was reasonably intact, the few leaks in her bottom already patched up, the water pumped out. The stepping and rigging of a jury mast would be a fairly simple matter, borrowing extra poles from the *Pallas*. The sail home, Jones anticipated, could be made with little difficulty.

Before leaving his prize, Jones visited the cockpit, where he found Surgeon Bannatyne and his assistants, their clothes smeared with blood, still busily tending the wounded. Crowded everywhere, bandaged, leaden-eyed men lay groaning or in a stupor or in merciful sleep. On deck as he was leaving Jones encountered the burial parties, preparing the dead for disposal in the North Sea. Each body was sewn up in a hammock or spare piece of canvas, and weighted with roundshot at the feet. Without ceremony, and with only a short prayer, two or three at a time were being slipped overboard.

It was late afternoon when Jones returned to the *Richard,* where Bragg and Cottineau told him there was simply no use in wasting further effort on the ship. It was even doubtful, they guessed, whether she would be able, if the winds picked up, to ride out the night. And the prisoners and wounded must be taken off immediately, since it was a task that would require some hours. At last, bowing to the inevitable, Jones ordered the evacuation begun. All hands not wanted at the pumps were to leave. Burial of the dead was to be halted. The bodies still aboard would be allowed to go down with the ship. It was just before 8 P.M. when Jones took his last look round the *Richard* and then formally transferred his flag to the *Serapis*. Pearson and Wright went with him.

Plying back and forth in the darkness through much of the night, small boats carried the wounded and the prisoners to other ships, while the pumping party tried to slow the flooding. It was nearly daylight when the last man was taken off. The pumping was then stopped and the work party left aboard turned to carry out Jones's final orders.

On each of the *Richard*'s three masts a complete set of sails was unfurled, and the jibs and staysails hoisted. All of the ship's pennants were run up and a new ensign was affixed at the stern, replacing the one shot off early in the fight. If the gallant old vessel was to be given to the sea, she would go down full-panoplied, robed in all her ravaged grandeur.

Midshipman Nathaniel Fanning, performing a last chore, went below to gather up whatever could be recovered of the stores and the officers' personal property, all of which had been piled in the hold with the furniture when the ship was cleared for action. "But good God!" he recalled. "What havoc! Not a piece of them could be found as large as a Continental dollar. The splinters and pieces of our ship were scattered about upon the deck in heaps." Twenty carpenters, the amazed Fanning estimated, sawing constantly for a week, could not have demolished the ship's interior so effectively.

When the signal was given to abandon ship, the last dozen men climbed down the side and into a waiting tender. A few minutes later it was alongside the *Serapis,* unloading. Fanning, about to haul himself aboard, was stopped by the voice of Captain

Jones calling instructions from above. He was to take three men, return to the *Richard,* and bring off a box of valuable papers left in Jones's cabin. There seemed no immediate danger of the ship going down, but Fanning was to hurry and was to take no undue risk. As it happened, that last-minute assignment made the young midshipman a privileged witness to the closing scenes of the *Bonhomme Richard*'s long career.

"I shaped my course for the poor old ship," Fanning recalled, "which was then about a mile from the *Serapis.* Arriving alongside, we found her lying nearly head to the wind, with her topsails aback, and the water running in and out of her lower deck ports. We shot along under her stern, where we were becalmed. I now ordered the oars to be got out, as I found by her motion, and by her being nearly under water, that she was on the point of sinking. This somewhat staggered me, and I ordered my men to pull at the oars with all their might. Finding our situation very dangerous, we got off about four rods from her, when she fetched a heavy pitch into a sea and a heavy roll, and disappeared instantaneously. The suction, together with the agitation of the waters, was so great that it was perhaps a minute before we could be certain whether we were above or under the water."

Watching from aboard the *Serapis,* hundreds of men, including many British, stared fascinated as the stricken vessel rolled under the boiling surface. Gunner John Kilby, one of the few who had escaped unmarked from the 18-pounder explosion, and whose eyes now brimmed unashamedly, always afterward remembered that final instant as "a most glorious sight!"

From his place on the *Serapis*'s quarterdeck, Captain Jones, feeling "inexpressible grief," took his last glimpse of his stout old warship, his heart stirred by the picture of the full-rigged vessel heeling to port and disappearing head foremost, all her pennants snapping in the rush of wind. As the bow submerged, the high poop deck rose up, briefly thrusting the red-white-and-blue ensign toward the sky.

Then the *Bonhomme Richard* was gone, the foaming turbulence gradually calming to a smooth eddy as small birds, crying shrilly, swooped and darted over her grave.

4

Reckoning

On 3 October, ten days after the sinking of the *Bonhomme Richard,* the American squadron reached Holland, where it anchored at Texel Island in the outer reaches of the Zuider Zee. Through a combination of bad weather and good fortune, and because a dozen Royal Navy ships had wasted their time in searching along Britain's coast, drawn on by rumors and false leads, the squadron had never come close to being intercepted.

At his first opportunity Jones sent a report of his operations to Benjamin Franklin in Paris. In it he accused Captain Landais of "highly criminal" conduct, involving cowardice, dereliction of duty and treason. Franklin, with the concurrence of the French authorities, promptly called Landais to Paris to make his reply in person, as a prelude to a court-martial. At the same time he asked Jones to prepare a written statement of charges, to be supported by depositions from concerned officers. These documents were in Franklin's hand by early November. They left no doubt that Jones's harsh judgment was fully shared by his men.

Specifying twenty-five counts of misconduct, these "Charges and Proofs" painted a damning picture of Landais's mad insubordination during the whole six weeks' cruise, culminating with the claim that he had fired, knowingly and maliciously, on the *Richard*. His purpose, the documents all but charged, was to cause Jones to strike his colors to the Englishman, giving Landais the opportunity to retake both ships, and allowing him to emerge as the hero of the day. Twenty-five officers of the squadron attested variously to the facts.

As regards Landais's neglect of duty and flagrant disobedience of orders, the case against him appeared inarguable. Yet, as it turned out, because of other circumstances he was never brought to trial. A dearth of American naval officers in France at the time made it necessary to transfer the site of the court-martial to the United States, causing a long delay. While crossing the Atlantic in the *Alliance,* Landais apparently became mentally deranged. His behavior toward both crew and passengers, among whom were several American Congressmen, grew steadily more alarming, until there arose actual fears for the ship's safety. In a short, bloodless mutiny, arranged and led by the Congressmen, Landais was removed from his post and confined under guard. Afterwards, as the result of an official hearing, he was dismissed from the Navy as unfit for command. He spent a good part of his later life denying all Jones's charges and grandly claiming to have played the decisive role in the famous battle.

Whether Landais really did deliberately attack the *Richard,* hoping either to sink her or hasten her surrender, or simply committed an unforgivable blunder, remains an open question. Benjamin Franklin, who knew Landais well, was inclined to doubt the charge of outright treachery, thinking it more likely that the excitable Frenchman had acted from cowardice and utter incompetence. Admiral Mahan, after a close study of all the circumstances, agreed with Franklin. Landais's firing on the *Richard,* he wrote, "was not due primarily, if at all, to a purpose to hurt her, but to timidity, personal or professional or both. This kept him out of action for a disgraceful length of time. . . . When driven by very shame to do something, this prevented his closing with the *Serapis.*"

Samuel Eliot Morison, on the other hand, was convinced of Landais's evil intentions. The hitting of the *Richard* by shot from the *Alliance,* he wrote, "cannot have been accidental, as Jones had his night recognition signals burning, the scene was illuminated by moonlight, gun flashes and fires; *Richard*'s topsides were painted black, and those of the *Serapis* bright yellow. The evidence is overwhelming that Landais did it on purpose."

In this marshaling of the evidence, however, Morison has overlooked the testimony of Captain Piercy as to the problem of identification caused by the smoke. Nor does he refer to the fact that if the *Richard* had been clearly, unmistakably outlined to the *Alliance*'s gunners, certainly none would have fired (a point first made by Franklin).

The question of the smoke, however, is not an easy one to evaluate. In the battle, the first pass of the *Alliance* occurred some fifteen or twenty minutes after Piercy, daunted by the curtain of smoke, had elected not to fire. That would put the first broad-side by the *Alliance* at just about 9 P.M., when the smoke must have been at its thickest. The second pass of the *Alliance,* with its two broadsides, took place about an hour later. Whether the smoke at that later period could have been so all-enveloping as it had been earlier is hard to decide. Still, it appears that there were some men on the *Alliance* who *were* able to distinguish the two ships in the smoke during that second pass. As Specification 20 of the "Charges" asserts, they "told Captain Landais at different times that he fired upon the wrong ship; others refused to fire." Even this is not conclusive, however, and only means that a few men caught a momentary glimpse of some revealing detail, allowing them to decide for themselves which ship was which. It could hardly have been an obvious or lengthy sighting, for in that case it is inconceivable that Landais could have ignored the warnings.

Landais's own defense of his actions never mentioned the smoke. He simply gave a different view of the maneuvering and flatly denied that any of his shot had hit the *Richard*. He had not engaged closely on the Englishman's free side, he explained, for fear of his shot carrying on through the enemy and into the *Richard*. Conversely, it was the danger of the American's shot reaching the *Alliance* that had kept him from trying to board. While that possibility existed, Landais must have known that in the circumstances the risk would have been more than acceptable—and it could have been quickly negated by a boarding from both sides.

But aside from the question of treasonable behavior, it seems that Landais did exhibit, even before the fight began, a professional prudence verging on cowardice. During the general chase, the *Alliance* spoke the *Pallas* and Landais counselled Cottineau that if the enemy proved to be a fifty-gun ship, "they must run away," an opinion which Cottineau rejected. True to his word, when Landais discovered that there were exactly fifty cannon bristling from the side of the English frigate, he ran away.

It was the shrewd John Adams, then in France, who perhaps best discerned the fatal flaw in Landais's character, a flaw which his eccentricities seemed designed to hide, and which bears on the question of his culpability. "There is in this man an inactivity and an indecision," wrote Adams, "that will ruin him; he is bewildered—an absent, bewildered man, an embarrassed mind." It does not seem likely that this unsettled, wavering personality could have conceived or carried out, entirely on his own and under the stare of his officers, so bold, so horrendous an act of treachery as a deliberate attack on his own commander's ship.

There the question must be left, unresolved, but with Landais condemned at the very least for shocking incompetence, a cowardice appalling to behold, and for shamefully dooming a large number of men on both sides to needless suffering and death.

Captain Pearson did not lose by his defeat. Rather he became, for a while at least, one of England's national heroes. Along with Captain Piercy, he was returned home in a prisoner exchange early in 1780. The two underwent a joint court-martial at Sheerness on 10 March, that year, and were found to have acted well and honorably. They had, said the court, "not only acquited themselves of their duty to their country, but have in the execution of such duty done infinite credit to themselves by a very obstinate defense against a superior force."

Pearson's share of the acclaim went far beyond anything accorded Piercy, obviously because he had been directly engaged with the notorious

John Paul Jones. Most impressively, he was awarded a knighthood, but there were many other honors. He was given the freedom of a dozen towns along the Yorkshire coast, and his birthplace, Appleby, commissioned a painting. The Corporation of Scarborough presented him with an elegant box, made of heart of oak and bearing the motto: "Life is but a span, glory is immortal. The property of the citizens, and the coasts, are defended. Under your auspices the sea is safe." Hull gave him a silver cup and two oak boxes. The Royal Exchange Commission, grateful that none of the convoy had been lost, tendered him a large and elegant cup, "of curious workmanship," the inscription declaring that Pearson and his men had "gained immortal honor." The Russian Company, which had large investments in the convoy, gave him a set of expensive silver plate, fittingly inscribed.

Part of the reason for this flood of honors—unusual for a man who had, after all, come out of the contest second best—was the fact that the details of the battle were not well understood in England until much later, had not even been well understood by the officers sitting on the court-martial. For a long while it was believed that the *Serapis* had fought continuously, not with Jones alone, but with two ships of the enemy, and had withstood impossible odds for more than three hours. It was Pearson himself, in his report to the Admiralty, who was the author of that mistake. While engaged with the *Bonhomme Richard,* Pearson had explained, "the largest of the two frigates kept sailing round us the whole action, and raking us fore and aft, by which means she killed and wounded almost every man on the quarter and main decks." The punishing broadsides from this second ship, he assured his superiors, had eventually forced his surrender.

No doubt Pearson was sincere in that claim, his confused memory of the chaotic scene having much enlarged the part played by the *Alliance*. Unfortunately, when the true facts became known in England a reaction set in. There were those who began to wonder whether it had really been so urgent a matter for Pearson to have struck when he did, remembering the inferiority and the shattered condition of his opponent.

Some later writers, less charitably, have interpreted Pearson's distortions as deliberate, and connived at by the British Admiralty. "The share taken by the *Alliance*," wrote Admiral Mahan, "flimsy as it was, was used by the British government of the day to give to this affair a color not reconcilable with the facts. That an 18-pounder, two-decked ship should have struck to a 12-pounder vessel, whose only claim to a second deck was the abortive battery of six eighteens, carried barely above the waterline, was a circumstance not to be admitted if it could be otherwise represented."

Yet in this view, it must be said, Mahan has left no room for what was the undoubted truth: To Pearson, the mere presence of the *Alliance*, whether sailing around the combatants or hove-to at a distance, at least had the appearance of posing a dire threat. And the existence of this threat played its part, however uncertain, justifiably or not, in his decision to strike his flag.

Another of the officers of the *Serapis,* Lt. Michael Stanhope, did not fare so well as his captain in the matter of reputation. Soon after the surrender a rumor went round among the English officers and crew accusing Stanhope of deserting his post under fire. So prevalent were the whispers that Pearson had the matter aired at the court-martial.

Supposedly, after climbing back aboard the ship and visiting the cockpit, Stanhope did not return to duty, but kept himself safely hidden during the remainder of the battle in purser Cockburne's cabin. It developed that the surgeon, William Bannatyne, was the sole source of the rumor. While working with the wounded in the cockpit, Bannatyne had glimpsed Stanhope entering the purser's cabin. About a half hour later, just prior to the surrender, he had seen the lieutenant leave to go above. Bannatyne himself was not present at the court-martial for questioning, having been assigned (rather hurriedly) to an outgoing vessel just before the trial. Stanhope was soon exonerated, however. The testimony of half a dozen witnesses, including Cockburne, made it clear that he had indeed returned to his post. But about a half hour later he had made a second visit to the cockpit, "in much pain," and had taken a second drink of wine in the purser's cabin. Bannatyne, seeing Stanhope leave the cabin after that second visit, and not having seen him in between, had too quickly assumed that he had been there all the while. On the evidence, the court decided that the insinuations against the lieutenant's reputation amounted to nothing more than "malice."

One of the men aboard the *Richard* also lost much of the honor that should have been his, though in this case it seems to have been largely the man's own doing. Seaman William Hamilton, who had flung that fatal grenade—and who was somehow wounded during the last half hour of the fight—for some reason became dissatisfied while the *Serapis* lay in Texel roadstead, and he deserted. With that act, he disappeared from history. All the many accounts of the battle written during the nineteenth century mention his heroic deed as the turning point, but the courageous seaman himself remained anonymous. Even Jones, in writing a subsequent account, didn't bother to search out Hamilton's identity but referred only to "the extraordinary intrepidity and presence of mind of a Scotch sailor posted in the maintop." It was not until 1905, when the manuscript of John Kilby's reminiscences came to light, that the name of William Hamilton was restored to its rightful place in the story. Regarding the man himself, regretfully, nothing further is known.

John Paul Jones, for his stunning triumph,

reaped honors almost equal to those of Pearson. He was invested by Louis XVI as a Chevalier of the *Ordre du Mérite Militaire,* and was also presented with a gold-hilted ceremonial sword by the King. One of France's leading sculptors, Jean Antoine Houdon, was commissioned to do a bust. The United States Congress voted him its thanks for a victory "so brilliant as to excite general applause," and later awarded him a special gold medal. George Washington, in a personal letter, assured him he had won "the admiration of all the world."

Yet perhaps it was none of these things that brought Jones his greatest satisfaction. The knowledge that all of America and France, and a good part of Europe, was ringing with his name and deeds must have afforded him a pleasure deeper than that provided by even the most exalted title or medal. He knew, as well as anyone, that an imperishable legend was in the making.

The part taken by Lt. Henry Lunt, with the pilot boat and the fifteen marines, remains one of the more obscure and controversial incidents of that memorable night. At just what point Lunt went aboard the *Serapis,* and whether he first boarded his own ship, is not known, but a reference by Lt. Dale places him on the deck of the English vessel within ten minutes or so of the surrender. Lunt himself left no extended account of the fighting, and gave only the barest explanation of his hesitation. "It being night," he wrote with true New England brevity, "I thought it not prudent to go alongside in time of action."

Judging from that clipped statement, and other bits of indirect evidence, it is nearly certain that Lunt stood entirely apart from the fighting for something like an hour, until all the guns were silenced, or until he saw the British flag come down in defeat. Thus the question is still asked today: Was Lt. Lunt's prudence wholly justified, or should he, no matter the danger, have taken his men back aboard the *Richard?*

Captain Jones, it seems, was at first inclined to censure Lunt for his failure to rejoin. But since the lieutenant afterwards continued to serve under Jones in his old capacity, his explanation to his commander must have been convincing at the time. And yet it seems that Jones was never quite able to rid himself of doubts. Years later, at any rate, he had become definite in his condemnation. Lunt and his men, Jones wrote in a passing reference, had been "mere spectators of the action, in which they took no interest, keeping themselves to windward and out of all danger."

Among subsequent writers, those qualified by experience to have an opinion, most avoided the subject, apparently believing that only someone present at the battle possessed the right to speak. Cooper, Mahan and Morison, in their otherwise circumstantial accounts, carefully sidestep any comment or conclusions. It was only Captain Mackenzie who allowed himself a voice, and he came close to leveling a charge of desertion. Lunt's conduct, Mackenzie insisted, "at least involved a great error of judgment, which no doubt he lived to repent."

Should Lt. Lunt have taken his men back aboard the *Richard* during, say, the final half hour of the battle, when the firing of the big guns had been much reduced and when the veil of smoke must have thinned? Remembering that Lunt held the important post of third officer, and that the shorthanded crew already on board was fighting for its life, the answer may seem inevitable. Yet who, lacking direct knowledge of all that transpired on that wild night, can say for sure?

More culpable than Lunt, at first sight, was the commander of the *Pallas*, Captain Cottineau. In taking it on himself to withdraw his ship from the line of battle ordered by Jones for the initial attack, he left his commodore to engage a superior enemy alone. Yet his explanation, strained as it may sound to modern ears, was accepted by Jones as sufficient —at least he chose so to accept it.

It seems that when the *Richard,* in full chase, altered course slightly to follow the westward-moving *Serapis,* the surprised Cottineau could think only that the English volunteers in Jones's crew had mutinied, perhaps had released the prisoners in the hold, had taken over the ship and were making for the shore. In that mistaken belief, exercising his independent authority, he had sheered off rather than risk an encounter on his own with the *Serapis*. When, some minutes later, the cannonading between the two big ships had commenced, Cottineau decided that his first duty lay in eliminating the threat posed by the *Countess*.

Jones afterwards praised Cottineau for taking the British sloop—though it required about two hours for him to do so—and said that he would be happy to serve with him again. For his part, Cottineau remained a supporter of Jones, calling him a good officer in his handling of men, and an excellent commander in action.

The English volunteers in Jones's crew, numbering perhaps fifty, contrary to the fears of some, made no attempt to mutiny. Nor did they raise any difficulty during the fight, but stood resolutely to their guns, suffering high casualties. Understandably, many among them fought with less than passionate conviction, and as soon as the battle ended, in the general confusion half a dozen managed to make their escape to shore in a dory. It was from the tales told by these escapees that there sprang the first and most lurid distortions about the battle and Jones's part in it.

Chief among the apocryphal stories that soon began to circulate was the assertion that Jones had personally shot and killed no less than seven men for desertion of their posts. He had also, it was said, turned his pistol on his own nephew, supposedly a lieutenant in his ship, "who he thought a little dastardly," and in preference to blowing out the lad's brains had terrorized him by peppering his shins. In time the facts and names changed, so that in another story the nephew became a certain "Lieutenant Grub," who was attempting to haul down the flag, and who was shot dead by his infuriated captain. Behind these tales, of course, was the actual incident that had occurred between Jones and Henry Gardner. Regarding the nephew, though Jones had no relatives aboard, there were two seaman on the *Richard* by that name. And there did exist a certain Midshipman Beaumont Groube, who, however, served well during the battle belowdecks and who, so far as is known, gave thought only to the glory to be won that day.

If the battle off Flamborough Head was not the bloodiest encounter in history between two ships under sail, there can have been few to equal it. Reflecting its chaotic nature, and the difficulty of making an exact count for some time afterward, the first reports of casualties were wildly above the mark. Pearson first believed that Jones had lost about three hundred dead and wounded. Jones felt that the English ship must have had at least a hundred killed, and such inflated totals continued to appear in later accounts. The most reliable figures put the combined dead and wounded for both ships at about 280, with about half of that number having lost their lives.

While there exist no complete or final lists for either British or Americans, from the few official documents available it is possible to derive a fairly close figure for the carnage that was wrought aboard each ship. This is especially true for the *Serapis,* whose original muster role is still preserved in London, along with a preliminary count set down by Captain Pearson.

On the *Serapis,* in the course of the battle, between thirty and forty men were killed outright. Nearly a hundred more sustained wounds, a great many of them serious, from burns and torn flesh to lost limbs. Before the squadron reached the Texel about a dozen of the wounded died, and within the following weeks perhaps another twenty succumbed. As late as February 1780, English sailors were still dying of their wounds.

The killed aboard the *Bonhomme Richard,* according to the only list available, numbered thirty-nine. But this figure refers only to the *Richard*'s crew and officers, overlooking what must have been a devastating loss among the French marines. The list also includes thirty-seven wounded, again ignoring the marines (this information presumably, was not available at the time Sherburne's list was compiled). Since Jones put his own estimate of total losses at well over a hundred (at first he feared that his casualties would run far more than 150, then later reduced that figure but without indicating any numbers), the French marines must have suffered some forty or more dead and wounded, perhaps a third of their strength.

As with the *Serapis,* the known dead aboard the *Richard* includes men killed in battle as well as those who died later of wounds, but the numbers of each is not known. Among the dead by nationality, while the greatest loss must certainly have been sustained by the French marines, the Portuguese, the Americans and the English volunteers also lost heavily.*

Midshipman Fanning, who luckily escaped without a scratch, in composing his memoir some twenty years afterward fell to musing on his lost comrades. The upwelling of old associations made suddenly vivid all that he had experienced as a young man. He recalled how, just before the *Richard* sank, he had taken his last look at "the mangled carcasses of the slain, especially between decks, where the bloody scene was enough to appal the stoutest heart." He remembered that, in the depression of the moment, an idea had visited him which made a little more bearable the thought of the awful price that the victory had exacted. "When I came to reflect that we were conquerors," he wrote, "and over those who wished to bind America in chains of everlasting slavery, my spirits revived, and I thought perhaps that some faithful historian would at some

* *See Appendix A for a list of the known dead and wounded aboard both ships.*

future period enroll me among the heroes and deliverers of my country."

Rest easy, Midshipman Fanning. You and your shipmates have not been forgotten. To have fought beside John Paul Jones aboard the *Bonhomme Richard* is to have won a high place on the rolls of your country's deliverers, its earliest heroes, and an enduring share in his glory.

End

Appendix

A
Roll of the Dead and Wounded, English and American

B
Notes And Sources

C
Bibliography

Appendix A

Roll of the Dead and Wounded, English and American

The earliest official enumeration of English casualties is a list compiled at the direction of Captain Pearson, dated 6 October 1779, three days after the squadron reached the Texel (original in PRO Admiralty I-2305). The totals, though not the names, from this list reached print in *The London Gazette,* 12 October 1779, and its figures have been frequently cited by later writers. But this list was made up at a time of great confusion, while the English were still scattered on the ships throughout the squadron. Some men were listed as dead who were merely unaccounted for, perhaps wounded, and in addition some of those listed as wounded later died. This is clear from comparison of Pearson's list with two other sources which so far seem to have been overlooked: a list of the dead entered in the *Serapis*'s muster role in February 1780 (PRO Admiralty 36-7908), and a preliminary list of wounded only, made up by Surgeon Bannatyne on 30 September 1779, while the squadron was still at sea (Sherburne, 133-4).*

The following roll of the English dead, based on analysis of all sources, includes sixty-one names. Concerning seven others, it is uncertain whether they were killed, or were wounded and survived, or were simply missing, hence they are given separately. To the list must be added seven or eight unnamed "Lascars" noted by Pearson in his list of 6 October.

The highest possible total for the killed aboard the *Serapis* thus can be set at seventy-five. By an affecting coincidence, about the same number of killed may quite probably be assigned to the *Richard*.

* *Bannatyne's list, as printed by Sherburne, contains sixteen names that do not appear in Pearson's list of 6 October. The discrepancy resulted from Sherburne's misreading, forty years after the fact, of the handwriting on the old documents. Pearson's list, written by an amanuensis, is very clear and I have collated the errors as follows (the name on Pearson's list is given first): Anderson—Addison; Bargett—Magot; Brownell —Brownhill; Cample—Campbell; Cross—Crow; Downs— Davis; Land—Paul; Lure—Lever; McLane—McLean; Medcalf—Metcalf; Murphle—Mersell; Rabbitch—Rubbish; Robelow—Pubbelon; Sexton—Seaton; Springett—Springale; Woods—Ward.*

The English Dead

Name	Quality	Whether died in battle or later
Alps, John	capt.'s servant	battle
Appleby, John	gunner	wounds
Ashby, John	seaman	burns
Ashworth, James	marine	wounds
Barber, Thomas	marine	battle
Booth, William	bosun's mate	wounds
Brown, William	master's mate	wounds
Bunting, William	seaman	battle
Busby, Thomas	seaman	battle
Chessy, Benjamin	seaman	battle
Cornish, Abraham	marine	burns
Cringle, William	seaman	wounds
Crozar, Richard	marine	wounds
Ellis, John	gunner	battle
Franks, Anthony	cockswain	wounds
Goodchild, James	seaman	battle
Hall, James	marine	battle
Hutchinson, Alexander	seaman	burns
Ingram, Robert	marine	burns
Jones, William	marine	battle
Jubb, Charles	master's mate	wounds
Kellow, William	marine	battle
Leveridge, Benjamin	seaman	battle

Name	Quality	Whether died in battle or later
Ludewig, George	midshipman	battle
Lure, George	carpenter's mate	wounds
McCachen, Charles	seaman	wounds
McLane, John	seaman	wounds
Mason, John	seaman	battle
Mein, Robert	seaman	battle
Middleton, John	marine corporal	battle
Mitchell, Alexander	gunner	wounds
Moore, William	seaman	battle
Morgan, Edward	marine captain	wounds
Mycock, William	clerk	wounds
Norton, Michael	capt.'s servant	battle
Oliver, John	marine	wounds
Omea, Archibald	seaman	wounds
Owen, William	quartermaster	battle
Parker, Thomas	seaman	battle
Parker, William	gunner	battle
Patterson, John	seaman	battle
Pearson, George	seaman	battle
Plaice, Edward	boatswain	wounds
Popplewell, William	midshipman	burns
Portsmouth, Abraham	quartermaster	burns
Postgate, George	pilot	battle

Name	Quality	Whether died in battle or later
Pritchard, Robert	carpenter	wounds
Purder, William	seaman	battle
Rich, John	seaman	battle
Rivers, Thomas	marine	burns
Robinson, Edward	seaman	wounds
Sarcher, William	marine	burns
Stevens, Joseph	marine	battle
Sullivan, Cornelius	seaman	battle
Taylor, Thomas	marine	battle
Vernon, Edward	quartermaster	wounds
Weekes, John	marine	battle
Weekes, Thomas	quartermaster	wounds
Wilkinson, John	gunner	wounds
Wilderspin, James	marine	battle

(The following seven men may have been killed, but may have been only wounded and survived.)

Aurendell, John	seaman
Dorman, Edward	seaman
Greening, William	seaman
Oakley, James	quartermaster
O'Hara, Andrew	seaman
Preston, John	marine
Rushton, Jonathan	marine

The English Wounded

Of the hundred or so wounded sustained by the *Serapis,* perhaps thirty subsequently died. Among the wounded who survived, fifty-seven names are known.

Name	Quality	Nature or location of wound
Anderson, Leonard	seaman	legs
Angell, Richard	seaman	hand
Anson, Robert	seaman	no record
Bargett, Stephen	seaman	back
Batchellor, Benjamin	seaman	no record
Bennett, William	seaman	badly burned
Brooks, Charles	seaman	shoulder
Brownell, John	master's mate	arm and side
Burton, Robert	seaman	no record
Cample, John	seaman	hand
Caw, James	seaman	badly burned
Clark, James	marine	wrist
Clark, William	seaman	thigh
Collins, James	petty officer	no record
Cross, William	marine	badly burned
Davies, Robert	marine	no record
Davis, Charles	seaman	haunch
Downs, Samuel	marine	arm and thigh
Fotheringham, John	seaman	no record

Name	Quality	Nature or location of wound
Gannell, John	seaman	no record
Garthside, Josiah	seaman	no record
Gordon, Samuel	seaman	no record
Guttridge, John	seaman	no record
Hale, Jeremiah	seaman	no record
Hook, Henry	seaman	arm and breast
Hudson, William	marine	shoulder
Hyslop, Thomas	gunner	badly burned
Kitchen, Walter	surgeon's mate	face burned
Land, John	marine	badly burned
Lawrence, John	seaman	badly burned
Lusty, James	marine	no record
McKnight, James	surgeon's mate	face burned
Mason, Richard	seaman	arm
Medal, James	seaman	no record
Medcalf, Charles	yeoman, deck	badly burned
Merriman, Richard	marine	no record
Mills, William	seaman	no record
Murphle, Thomas	seaman	arm and thigh
Murphy, Jeremiah	seaman	badly burned
Ozard, Robert	sailmaker	burned
Pickersgill, Benjamin	seaman	badly burned
Powell, John	seaman	no record
Rabbitch, Thomas	seaman	shoulder
Richardson, George	seaman	no record

Name	Quality	Nature or location of wound
Robelow, William	petty officer	back
Robertson, John	seaman	legs
Robinson, William	seaman	no record
Rogers, William	seaman	arm
Sandwell, Thomas	surgeon's mate	badly burned
Sexton, Richard	seaman	badly burned
Spalding, Thomas	boy	badly burned
Springett, James	seaman	badly burned
Stanhope, Michael	2nd Lt.	burned
Thompson, Peter	seaman	no record
Weightman, Samuel	marine Lt.	arms

The Sherburne biography of Jones (1825) includes what purports to be a complete roster of the *Richard*'s complement, exclusive of the French marines, in which the dead and wounded are identified. The roster is given as from an "official source," which is left unspecified. Sherburne did have ready access to government documents (he served in the Navy Department), and appears to have been a careful if uninspired compiler. However, while he lists forty-two men as "killed," and thirty-eight as "wounded," a comparison with the *Richard*'s muster role (see the Bibliography under Middlebrook) shows that he has again confused some names. The true totals, it appears, should be thirty-nine and thirty-seven, not counting the French marines. There is no way to tell finally, of course, whether Sherburne's totals are complete even as to the crew.

Analysis of the muster role and Sherburne's listings yields another pathetic fact: Five or six of the dead, who are identified as "seaman," were actually teenaged powder boys, among the fifteen or so who had been given shipboard promotions in order to strengthen the depleted crew.

The American Dead

(Not including the French marines)

Name	Quality	Nationality
Antoine, Alexander	seaman	Portuguese
Antoine, Louis	seaman	Portuguese
Antoine, Manuel	seaman	Portuguese
Bailey, Nathaniel	seaman	American
Baterga, Jacques	seaman	unknown
Brewster, Josiah	armorer	American
Carreau, Perry	seaman	unknown
Carswell, Joshua	master's mate	American
Clarke, Thomas	seaman	English
Corrisque, Antoine	seaman	Portuguese
Crooks, Jeremiah	seaman	English

Name	Quality	Nationality
Davis, Thomas	armorer	English
Dougherty, Robert	seaman	English
Frerry, John	seaman	unknown
Gorrica, John	seaman	unknown
Harroway, George	seaman	Scotch
Hill, Robert	seaman	English
Ignace, Vincent	seaman	Portuguese
Joseph, Joachim	seaman	Portuguese
Loley, Stephen	seaman	American
Longstaff, Michael	quartermaster	American
Loria, Jacques	seaman	unknown
Macarthy, Thomas	quarter gunner	Irish
Mare, Joseph	seaman	Portuguese
Martin, Henry	seaman	American
Mason, Andrew	boy	American
Maurda, Joseph	seaman	Portuguese
Murphy, John	gunner	Irish
Murphy, William	boy	American
Nicholson, James	seaman	American
Perkins, Francis	seaman	American
Physic, William	carpenter's mate	English
Ridway, John	seaman	English
Rodrique, Joseph	seaman	Portuguese
Steel, Robert	quartermaster	English
Sylvestre, Antoine	seaman	Portuguese
Tomis, Lewis Role	seaman	unknown
Turner, Thomas	boatswain	English
Williams, John	quartermaster	English

The American Wounded

(Not including the French marines)

Name	Quality	Nationality
Brown, John	seaman	English
Burnet, John	seaman	American
Clarke, William	sailmaker	American
Connor, John	seaman	Irish
Cullingwood, John	seaman	English
Dale, Richard	1st Lt.	American
Euroney, Hugh	seaman	unknown
Francisque, Antoine	seaman	Portuguese
Furlong, Lawrence	seaman	Irish
Gardner, Henry	chief gunner	American
Hamilton, William	seaman	Scotch
Hammet, Thomas	seaman	American
Holliday, John	boy	American
Hughes, Richard	seaman	unknown
Johnston, George	seaman	Norwegian
Jordan, John	seaman	English
Lenn, James	seaman	English
Lyon, Robert	boy	American
Lyons, John	seaman	unknown
McCullough, William	boy	American
McIntyre, John	seaman	Irish
McKinley, James	seaman	American
McMichan, James	boy	American
Mayrant, John	midshipman	American
Mease, Matthew	purser	American

Name	Quality	Nationality
Peterson, Charles	seaman	Swedish
Potter, Thomas	midshipman	American
Simpson, William	boy	American
Smith, Aaron	seaman	unknown
Swain, Daniel	seaman	American
Thomas, John	cook	American
Trefathen, George	seaman	unknown
Upham, Robert	boy	American
Wat, Thomas	seaman	English
Wiera, Joseph	seaman	Portuguese
Williams, Richard	seaman	unknown
Wythe, Thomas	seaman	English

Appendix B

Notes And Sources

In these Notes I have not felt it necessary to give sources for those more general facts which are the common property of Jones biography. I have done so, however, with every element, large and small, of the battle itself and its aftermath. Thus, each statement of fact, or interpretation of fact, is herein for the first time linked directly to the testimony of eyewitnesses. And on each particular point, all pertinent primary documents are cited, not just those on which I mainly base my conclusions.

While I have consulted all the principal secondary accounts, these are not always cited below since it is the primary material which has controlled my picture. Secondary sources are noticed only where they have added a dimension or aided my understanding.

Mingled with these citations will be found some further remarks, observations and sundry bits of information which seem valuable or at least interesting.

The order of items in these Notes corresponds with the sequence of the narrative. Thus even without the clutter of page references little effort is needed to locate any desired item.

References are given in shortened form and may be more fully identified by recourse to the Bibliography. For those sources that are repeatedly cited the following abbreviations have been used:

JR—Jones's report of 3 October 1779, to Benjamin Franklin.

PR—Pearson's report of 6 October 1779, to the Admiralty.

NWR—*Niles's Weekly Register,* June–July 1812, containing a later account of the battle by Jones.

TPC—Transcript, Pearson court-martial.

Part One
Rendezvous at Flamborough Head

Arrival of the *Serapis* on the English coast: PR 93; Ms. letter of Pearson, 23 September 1779, written aboard the *Serapis* just prior to his receiving information about Jones's presence (original in PRO Admiralty 1-2305). Also Mahan, *Scribner's* 206–7; Morison 226–7.

Letter sent aboard the *Serapis* from bailiff of Scarborough: A copy of this letter, enclosing a copy of another warning note from observers at Sunderland, is in PRO Admiralty 1-2305. Probably written in haste, it is brief and makes no mention of Jones's threatened actions the week before at Leith and Newcastle. But this important information, so recently the talk of England's channel coast, would certainly have been told to Pearson by the messenger.

Incidents of Jones's earlier cruise (April 1778): Halliday, *American Heritage,* June 1970; *Edinburgh Memoirs,* 56–75; Morison 138–154.

First sighting of Jones's squadron by the convoy: PR 93–4; the lone merchant ship that rounded the Head is nowhere identified as the actual vessel later spotted by the American squadron to the south, but it is an obvious conclusion from the evidence. In this connection see JR 145, and Sherburne 128.

The *Serapis,* her officers and crew: Cooper, *Lives,* 62–3; Mahan, *Scribner's* 207; Lorenz 292; Morison 226; muster roll of the *Serapis* in PRO Admiralty 36-7908.

According to Morison, the *Serapis*'s 18-pounders were not in the best condition, their worn vents allowing too much of the force of the gunpowder explosion to escape. Morison's source (not cited by him) is a letter from Pearson to the Admiralty written 19 July 1779 (PRO Admiralty 1-2305). However, in this letter Pearson complains not of the eighteens having enlarged vents, but of the 9-pounders in the upper deck battery. Moreover, his purpose in writing was to get these old guns exchanged for newer ones and his request may well have been honored.

Background of Captain Pearson: *Naval Chronicle,* XXIV, 1810, 353–61; *Naval Atlantis,* London, 1789, 29–30; *Dictionary of National Biography,* VI, 619–20. The fact that Pearson suffered from rheumatism in spring 1779 has not before appeared in print. The evidence is in two notes he wrote the Admiralty, in February and April, when the *Serapis* was fitting out. In the first he writes: "Being still much afflicted with the rheumatism . . . I am to request that their Lordships will be pleased to grant me a fortnight or three weeks leave for the recovery of my health." In the second, written five weeks later, he says he still has not recovered and requests another fortnight (PRO Admiralty 1-2305).

Pursuit of the small brig by Jones's squadron: JR 145; NWR 296; Cooper, *Lives,* 60; Middlebrook 45.

Jones's height has been estimated at 5'7", though Morison (17) thinks he stood no more than 5'5", pointing out that a number of contemporaries referred to him as "little." Cooper (*Lives,* 11), who had his information from Dale, says simply that he was "of the middle stature." The *Edinburgh Memoirs* (393) pictures him as "about the middle size, slightly made, but active and agile, and in youth capable of considerable exertion and fatigue."

That the cruise of the *Bonhomme Richard*

Squadron was to terminate by 1 October 1779 is in Lorenz 266. While the purpose of the cruise was as I have given it—harassment of the enemy homeland—in the background lay a broader purpose, one which I have not treated because it proved to have no real link with the course of Jones's actions or with the battle. This was the planned invasion of southern England by a combined French-Spanish Fleet during July-August 1779, for which Jones originally was intended to create a diversion to the north. But this Combined Fleet, principally because of rampaging sickness among the crews, gave up and sailed away some three weeks before Jones encountered the *Serapis*. Also, the *Bonhomme Richard* Squadron initially included three other ships, all privateers voluntarily with Jones. I have not mentioned these because, long before the battle, they deserted the squadron to prowl in search of more lucrative prey.

"To go in harm's way . . ."—Lorenz XIII.

"If I survive . . ."—Morison 186.

"I have never served but . . ."—*Edinburgh Memoirs* 143.

"Eccentricities and irregularities . . ."—Lorenz 256.

Jones's character and personality have long been the subject of discussion. My own impression was formed after study of his whole career, and in the light of estimates made by both his contemporaries and later writers. His most unattractive trait, it appears, was a disinclination to give sufficient credit to those who served under him, a tendency which once received a mild rebuke from Benjamin Franklin. "If you should observe an occasion," Franklin chided, "to give your officers and friends a little more praise than is their due, and confess more fault than you can justly be charged with, you will only become the sooner for it a great captain." My own impression is that Jones did not deliberately withhold praise, but simply overlooked it in the continual restless heats of his own driving ambitions, a not uncommon tendency in self-made men. Regarding the battle with the *Serapis* he certainly did single out a number of men (mentioned below) for special notice; though it is true that, even here, he might have been more official and more particular about names and deeds.

An interesting summing up of the Jones character by James Fenimore Cooper affords some idea of the extent to which the image of the great captain, a half century after his death, still puzzled and fascinated:

> There can be no question that Paul Jones was a great man. By this we mean far more than an enterprising and dashing seaman. The success which attended exploits affected by very insufficient means, forms the least portion of his claims to the character. His mind aimed at high objects, and kept an even pace with his elevated views . . . all the cruises of the man indicated forethought, intrepidity and resources. Certainly no sea captain under the American flag, Preble excepted, has ever yet equaled him in these particulars.

That Jones had many defects of character is certain. They arose in part from temperament, and in part from education. His constant declaration of the delicacy of his sentiments, though true in the main, were in a taste that higher associations in youth would probably have corrected. There was, however, a loftiness of feeling about him, that disinclined him equally to meanness and vulgarity. . . .

There was something in the personal character of Jones that weakened his hold on his contemporaries, though it does not appear to have ever produced a want of confidence in his services or probity. . . . His cards bore the simple, but proud name of "Paul Jones," without any titles or official rank. His associations, too, were unquestionably high at one period of his life . . . the Duke of Dorset, the English Ambassador at Paris, freely received him, and he is said to have lived on terms of intimacy with Lord Wemys, Admiral Digby and others of like condition. . . .

Glory, he constantly avowed, was his aim, and there is reason to think he did not mistake his own motives in this particular. It is perhaps to be regretted that his love of glory was so closely connected with his personal vanity; but even this is better than the vanity which is sought as an instrument of ruthless power . . . but it appears certain that his defects were relieved by high proofs of greatness. (*Lives,* 108–12)

"I consider this officer . . ."—Jefferson to Wm. Carmichael, 12 August 1788, quoted in Lorenz XIV.

"It was impossible . . ."—Lorenz 399.

"The only mistress to . . ."—*Edinburgh Memoirs* 353.

For some speculation on the means of Jones's entry into America, and on his acquirement of that name, see Morison 420–23.

"The Concordat" under which Jones commanded the squadron is mentioned in most biographies, but it is most fully covered in Lorenz 260–61, 271–2. "At any other time and in all other circumstances," Jones explained afterward, "I should have rejected these conditions with disdain; I saw the danger which I ran . . . I took the resolution to expose myself to every peril." The document was presented for his signature almost at the last moment before sailing (JR 149).

The *Richard* and its crew: Sherburne 140–1; Middlebrook 3–16; Lorenz 252–8; Morison 186–93, 200–207. The *Richard*'s 18-pounder battery, carried just above the waterline, was originally intended for use only on the calm waters of harbors. In rough water, with the rolling ship's open gunports dipping beneath the waves, the eighteens would have been useless. They were employed against the *Serapis* only because of the exceeding calm that prevailed (NWR 296).

"Revenge sometimes is quite . . ."—Kilby 28.

The English prisoners on the *Richard:* Estimates of the actual number of Jones's prisoners vary widely, anywhere from one hundred to five hundred. But these prisoners would have been mostly the officers and petty officers taken off merchant prizes; and since the number of prizes taken prior to the battle was about fifteen, most of them small vessels, the total number of prisoners could not have been much above a hundred.

"I wish for none but . . ."—Lorenz 254.

Background of Lt. Dale: *Port Folio,* June 1814; Sherburne 361–3; Cooper, *Lives,* 233–64; *Dictionary of American Biography* I, 32–3; *Penn. Mag. of Hist. and Bio.,* IV, 1880, 494–500. That Dale had the respect and even affection of the men under him is a fact recorded by Midshipman Fanning: "While I sailed with him he was beloved by his brother officers, and the ship's crews. And to use a sailor's phrase, 'he was a clever, good-natured sea officer'; and was always diligent in his duty, which gained him the applause of his superiors. He was engaging in conversation, with all ranks of people, polite in his manners, and a good companion. He had none of that haughty, overbearing, domineering spirit about him, which is so frequently seen on board of English ships of war in officers of his rank toward their inferiors, especially the poor tars." Dale's later career took him near the pinnacle of the U. S. naval command. After the Revolution he was made captain of one of the first six frigates built by America. Later he took charge of the Mediterranean Squadron during the time of the Barbary pirates, with the rank of commodore. He died in retirement in Philadelphia in 1825.

"His bosom now beat high . . ."—*Port Folio* 504.

The *Richard*'s ten midshipmen: John Linthwaite, Robert Coram, John Mayrant, Nathaniel

Fanning, Beaumont Groube, Thomas Potter, Benjamin Stubbs, William Daniel, Thomas Lundy, Reuben Chase (having been assigned to a prize a few days before, Chase did not take part in the battle). Regarding the first four, Jones later wrote that they had proved efficient and brave, and that their conduct in the battle did them "great honor." (Sherburne 167, 169, 173.) This does not exclude the others from the possibility of like commendation, only that Jones seems not to have had an opportunity for similar comment on them. Also aboard, as liaison officer between Jones and the French marines, was Captain Alexander Dick of the American marines, who is mentioned in Kilby (25) as having previously been a fellow prisoner of war in Portsea Jail.

Regarding the *Richard*'s surgeon, Lawrence Brooke, Morison (203) has made an unfortunate misstatement which cries out for correction. Morison asserts: "Midshipman Fanning wrote that Dr. Brooke was more butcher than surgeon." But what Fanning actually wrote was to the exact contrary: "The fact was, we had but one surgeon in the squadron who really knew his duty, and that was Dr. Brooke, a Virginian; this man was as bloody as a butcher from the commencement of the battle until towards night of the day after." (Fanning 53–4.)

"To depress rather than . . ."—Dale in Sherburne 127.

Captain Pearson left no record of his calculations on the force of the approaching American squadron. About the earlier moments he merely says that "from their keeping end upon us, on bearing down, we could not discern what colours they were under." (PR 94.) But thoughts similar to those I have sketched must necessarily have occupied Pearson's mind at the time, since the gauging of an enemy's strength and probable mode of attack was almost a commander's first concern as battle became imminent.

Pearson nailing the Red Ensign to the mast: Dale in Sherburne 128; Fanning 44; Mackenzie 179.

Sighting and chase of the English convoy by Jones's squadron: Middlebrook 44, 45–6; JR 145; NWR 296; Kilby 30; *Port Folio* 506; Cooper, *Lives,* 60–1. Dale himself recorded the fact that he was asleep below when the convoy was first sighted, and that he was awakened by the noise (Sherburne 126). From this I have assumed that he was on watch the night before. He has made a slip of memory, however, in saying that on coming topside he inquired of an English coasting pilot (taken captive some days before) what fleet it was, receiving the reply that it was "the Baltic fleet under convoy of the *Serapis* of 44 guns, and the *Countess of Scarborough* of 20 guns." The pilot might have guessed that it was the Baltic convoy, but he could hardly have known who the escorts were. Jones himself did not know the identity of his antagonist until after the battle (JR 147). In NWR 296, Jones does claim to have known, but that statement was written about six years after the first. In this he has made the same error of memory as Dale, adding to an earlier fact bits of information learned only later.

The conduct of Pierre Landais prior to the battle: "Charges and Proofs" against Landais in Sherburne 162–5. One small incident, recalled later by Matthew Mease (his deposition in Sherburne 174–5), will illustrate how blatant was Landais's insubordination. During the early part of the cruise Jones signaled orders for a meeting of captains aboard the *Richard*. Cottineau and Ricot were promptly rowed over from their vessels, but Landais made no response at all. Jones then gave Mease a note to carry personally to Laidais. Mease continues:

> I went on board the *Alliance* and delivered Capt. Landais the letter, which he took with him to the cabin, and in a few minutes returned and delivered me another for Capt. Jones; this I brought instantly on board and delivered to him. It contained a second refusal on the part of Capt. Landais, and very much offended the gentlemen who had politely obeyed the signal and were then waiting for him. Capt. Jones, chagrined by the obstinacy of that officer, would have proceeded to the business he had in view, without paying any further attention to him; but being still anxious to have his opinion on, and approbation of the measure, conjointly with the other officers of the squadron, a further attempt to obtain his company was resolved on. For this purpose, at the desire of Capt. Jones, Capt. Cottineau, M. Chamillard and myself went on board the *Alliance,* to try the effect of persuasion on Capt. Landais; but in vain did those gentlemen represent to

him the absolute necessity there was for his joining in consultation with his brother officers; that the good of the service demanded his compliance, as an enterprise of some moment was to be decided on; but alas! in vain did they waste an hour and more in arguments to this end—in vain did they attempt to persuade him—in vain did they entreat him—in vain did they tell him what he had to dread from the consequences of his obstinately persisting to disobey the orders of his commanding officer. Instead of paying polite attention to the advice given him, he, on the contrary, not only disregarded it, but gave himself the liberty to speak of Capt. Jones in terms highly disrespectful and insolent, and said he would see him on shore, when they must kill one or the other.

More than one commentator has wondered why Jones gave Landais so much rope, especially when Landais made such wild statements as the one above, why he did not clamp him in irons long before the battle. The answer is the hampering "Concordat" under which he held command, an instrument which left the scope of his authority in doubt. Also there were obvious political and diplomatic questions involved concerning an ally. And it must be remembered that the ethics of command of the eighteenth century were not those rigid rules that prevail today, especially at sea. For more on Landais, see below, pp. 154, 163.

Jones's call for Line of Battle: JR 145; Sherburne 163; Cooper, *Lives,* 64.

"Even as in a millpond . . ."—Fanning 36.

The preliminary hailing between the ships:

PR 94; Fanning 36; Middlebrook 45–6; Kilby 31; Sherburne 126; Cooper, *Lives,* 65.

Part Two
The Battle

That Jones replied personally to the *Serapis*'s hails, unusual for a commodore, is stated in Kilby 31. At the beginning of the battle Kilby was serving one of the *Richard*'s 18-pounders, which would have put him almost directly below Jones on the quarterdeck. "Before the action commenced," Kilby explained, "everything was so silent that a man could easily hear everything said." After the explosion of the eighteens, from which Kilby escaped unharmed, he joined the crews at the quarterdeck guns.

Opening broadsides of both ships: JR 145; PR 94; Dale in Sherburne 126; Kilby 31; Fanning 36.

The accidental explosion of the *Richard*'s 18-pounders: JR 146; NWR 296; Fanning 36; Kilby 31; *Port Folio* 508. There is a question as to whether the explosion occurred on the first or second broadside. The weight of the evidence, I feel, favors the second.

Casualties among the marines on the poop deck: JR 146; Fanning 37.

Jones's decision to board: JR 145; NWR 296–7. "As I had to deal with an enemy of greatly superior force," Jones explained, "I was under the necessity of closing with him, to prevent the advantage which he had over me in point of maneuver." (The advantage in combined force and maneuver, he meant.) A curious oversight by previous writers on the battle concerns Jones's boarding plans. While all report the initial decision, and the attempts to grapple, in describing the subsequent action they lose sight of Jones's purpose, as if thereafter he was content to trade broadsides. The truth is, of course, that throughout the action Jones continually hoped to effect a boarding, and was repeatedly delayed or interrupted in that effort. The reasons for the delays I have tried to show in the narrative, especially the two passes by the *Alliance*.

Jones's orders to the fighting tops: That Jones gave such orders is evident from many allusions, and from subsequent events, though the fact is not stated in so many words. See Morison 232, 234; Lorenz 300.

Maneuvering of the ships prior to the grappling: JR 145; PR 94–5; Dale in Sherburne 126; Cooper 66–9; Fanning 36–7; Mackenzie 180–3; Mahan 208; Morison 229–31. Understandably, there has always been a good deal of disagreement, even among experts, over the exact moves made by the two ships. Descriptions provided by the participants, including Jones and Pearson, do not always agree in specifics, and lack much pertinent detail. My study of all original sources, in light of the ideas of later commentators, leads me to agree for the most part with Morison. I part company with him most seriously only in regard to the first collision, which he pictures as between the *Richard*'s port bow, and the *Serapis*'s starboard quarter, and as a definite attempt to board. "This was a very disadvantageous position," Morison remarks, "from which to carry an enemy ship by boarding . . . the English sailors repulsed the boarders, and Jones sheered off." My view, agreeing with Mahan, is that the contact took place between the *Richard*'s starboard bow and the *Serapis*'s port quarter, and was an accident, not a real boarding attempt.

"Wore short round upon . . ."—Sherburne 127.

Jones's laying of the *Serapis* athwart hawse: JR 145; NWR 296–7; PR 94–5; Dale in Sherburne 127; Cooper 68–9; Mahan 208–9. I see this maneuver not as a simple attempt to rake the enemy by the bow, its usual interpretation, but as a desperate effort to intercept the *Serapis*'s progress, halting her by a deliberate collision. In the light winds this would have been quite feasible, though perhaps only a captain of Jones's skill and daring would have attempted such a move. His own brief description of his purpose implies more than a simple attempt to rake: "It was my intention to lay the B.H.R. athwart the enemy's bow, but as that operation required great dexterity in the management of both sails and helm, and some of our braces being shot away, it did not succeed exactly to my wishes." Elsewhere he says more precisely, "I had recourse to a dangerous expedient, to grapple with the *Serapis*" (NWR 296), which again implies something out of the ordinary, in fact a grapple. There would have been no unusual danger in a simple attempt to rake by the bow.

"Well done, my brave lads . . ."—Fanning 38.

"It is no time for swearing . . ."—Fanning 38.

That Jones himself made a line fast from the *Serapis* is recorded in Fanning 38; NWR 297.

The grappling: JR 145; PR 94–5; Sherburne 127; Fanning 38; Kilby 31; Cooper 69–71; Mackenzie 182–3; Mahan 209; Morison 230–3.

"Thursday evening we were . . ."—Seitz 53. A second armchair viewer of the fight, of whom there is record, was a certain Samuel Beilby of Scarborough, who wrote the Duke of Rutland a couple of days later: "On thursday night, from about seven to eleven o'clock, I was an eyewitness from Osbaldiston's house of an engagement opposite to it in Filey Bay off Flamborough Head, between Paul Jones' squadron . . . and two of our own ships." The letter contains a few details, all obviously the result of rumor and all incorrect. (Hist. MSS. Comm., 12th Report, Part IV, Rutland MSS., Vol. 3, London 1894.)

Actions of Captain Piercy with the *Countess:* His report to Pearson, dated 4 October 1779, in Seitz 98–99.

Lt. Lunt's entry on the battle scene and his observations are in his deposition in Sherburne 170–1. Lunt does not say that he urged Ricot to enter the fight, or that Ricot refused; but there is no doubt that Lunt spoke the *Vengeance* and was told by Ricot to use the small pilot boat to take his own men aboard the *Richard*. My reading of all the circumstances convinces me that Lunt's purpose in running up alongside the *Vengeance* was as I describe. For more on this point see below, pp. 165–166.

The movement of the *Alliance* toward the battle at this time is recorded by Lunt in Sherburne 171.

"Unremitting fury . . ."—JR 145.

The spontaneous boarding attempt by both sides just after the grapple has usually been overlooked in later accounts. But that it did in fact take place, and about as I have described, is clear from separate statements in NWR 297; *Port Folio* 506; Kilby 31; Fanning 39; Lorenz 299.

That the sponge and rammer handles of the *Richard*'s gun crews, perhaps also of the *Serapis,* were at times thrust in through the enemy gunports is reported by Dale in Sherburne 127, and Cooper, *Lives,* 71.

Jones taking the place of the wounded Mease: JR 146; NWR 297; also Mease's deposition in Sherburne 175. Jones's difficulty in training the extra 9-pounder on the *Serapis*'s mainmast is not mentioned in the documents or secondary accounts, but is indicated by the relative positions of the two ships.

First pass of the *Alliance:* NWR 297; Middlebrook 46; Sherburne 163–4, 171; Mackenzie 186–7; Cooper, *Lives,* 73; Mahan, *Scribner's,* 211; Morison 235.

Death of Master's Mate Joshua Carswell: Linthwaite deposition in Sherburne 173; Middlebrook 3; Cooper, *Lives,* 75.

The reports of Dale and Gunnison to Jones: JR 146; Kilby 31. Jones does not say that Dale reported to him personally, only that the 12-pounders "were entirely silenced and abandoned." I have assumed that Dale himself would have brought this disheartening news to his commander.

"For God's sake, Captain . . ."—Lorenz 304; also Morison 235. The report of the incident appeared in the London *Public Advertiser,* 30 October 1779, which quoted one of the escapees from the *Richard.*

The shooting of the last English sharpshooter in the *Serapis*'s foretop: Fanning 38. As Fanning remembered it, he himself gave the order to the *Richard*'s maintopmen to fire. He may well have; but Lt. Stack was in charge of that party, and he received particular commendation from Jones afterward (see below p. 154). That Fanning served in the maintop is clear from the documents, yet Morison for some reason has placed him in command of the foretop. No one on the *Richard*'s foretop, however, could have had a clear view of the enemy's foretop, at least half a ship's length away, and curtained by the bulky, clewed-up mainsails as well as the spread topsails.

William Hamilton's exploit: Curiously, Jones in his first report makes no mention of Hamilton and his grenade throwing, or of the resulting explosion. When he wrote that report, ten days had passed since the battle, but they were days of much anxiety, and nine of them were spent at sea running for a safe port, under a jury-rigged mainmast. It is possible that the facts about Hamilton had not yet been ascertained, or at least not yet reported to Jones. However, Jones does give full credit to the exploit, though omitting to supply Hamilton's name, in NWR 298. Pearson himself, not knowing the source of the grenade, had this to say: "Either from a hand grenade being thrown in at one of our lower ports, or from some other accident, a cartridge all the way aft, blew up the whole of the people and officers that were quartered abaft the mainmast." (PR 95.) Kilby, though some of his details about the incident are in error, identifies the man who crawled out on the yardarm as William Hamilton, a name which also occurs in Sherburne's roster of the *Richard* (145), as among the wounded, and in the roster in Middlebrook (8), where he is listed as "seaman." Kilby notes further: "Hamilton, for his good conduct, was made Master's Mate, but though he fought so manfully, he ran away from the ship in the Texel."

Hamilton was not the only one of the *Richard*'s crew to desert from the *Serapis* in the Texel. On the evening of 14 October, some twenty men, most of them English, stole a boat and made for the shore in neutral Holland. Pursued by a patrol under Lt. Stack, about half were captured and brought back. Among those who succeeded in getting away were two gunners, both English, Arthur Randall and Robert Stevens, and two Irish seamen who had been wounded in the battle, Aaron Smith and John McIntyre. (Barnes 32; Sherburne 141–5; Middlebrook 4–16).

The explosion is also recalled by Dale in Sherburne 126, in *Port Folio* 510, and in Cooper, *Lives,* 77, though in none of these is Hamilton's name given. See also, Fanning 43.

The numerous fires aboard the *Serapis* are specifically mentioned by Pearson as his greatest danger in PR 95. Lt. Wright later testified (TPC 3) that the ship at one time "was on fire in eight or nine places, in short the starboard side was all in a blaze."

Master Wheatley sent below by Pearson: TPC 16. Wheatley says that he was sent down to encourage Stanhope and his men "two or three times before the explosion." I calculate that the third trip down occurred just before the grenade went off. The devastation caused by the explosion is detailed in Sherburne 128; PR 95; Cooper, *Lives,* 78; TPC 5.

Seaman Ozard and Lt. Stanhope overboard: TPC 8–14.

The surrender of the *Countess,* as nearly as can be judged, took place soon after 9:30, or just prior to the explosion aboard the *Serapis.* Piercy later said that he had engaged the *Pallas* for almost two hours, starting about 7:30. (Seitz 98.) He reported four men killed and twenty wounded.

The *Alliance* began its second move toward

the battle scene, according to analysis of the observations of Lunt, Fanning and Jones, just before 10 P.M. Pearson certainly would have noted her approach.

"The water which we had . . ."—Fanning 42.

"A person must have been an . . ."—JR 148.

"I now thought the battle . . ."—JR 147.

The second pass of the *Alliance:* JR 147; NWR 297; Fanning 43–4; Kilby 32, 41; Middlebrook 46; Sherburne 167–173; Mahan 211; Lorenz 302–3; Morison 234–5. The second broadside fired during this second pass, according to Midshipman Linthwaite, came at a time "when the *Alliance* was not more than three points abaft the *Bonhomme Richard*'s beam." (Sherburne 164.) Regarding the *Alliance*'s raking of the *Richard* by the bow, Midshipman Coram was of the opinion that "had the *Alliance* come half the distance nearer the *Serapis* than she did, she might have cleared the enemy's deck, and not have raked the *Bonhomme Richard*." (Sherburne 169.) Midshipman Mayrant agreed that Landais "might have come half as near again without any danger of running foul of us." (Sherburne 168.) In these assertions the two intended to convict Landais of cowardice, at least.

"I beg you will not sink us . . ."—Stack in Sherburne 172. Jones's later praise of Stack's service in the maintop was unstinted. He said that the Irishman's performance was essential to the victory, and it was largely through his recommendation that Stack was later made a captain in his French regiment, with an annuity for life from Louis XVI (Sherburne 173).

Lt. Stack calling for his men to fire on the *Alliance:* Sherburne 172.

The officers who asked Jones to strike: JR 147; Lorenz 304; Morison 236.

The Gardner-Gunnison incident: Fanning 41–2; Kilby 32; JR 146; NWR 297; Lorenz 304–5; Morison 236. Fanning relates that Gardner recovered from the blow of the pistol, but that he was later reduced by Jones to the rank of ordinary seaman, "and that was all the punishment he received for his crime." The master at arms, Burbank, was put in irons, but was later released (Barnes, 29). It appears that Jones's lenient view of the incident rested on the fact, as he said, that both Gardner and Gunnison had previously been slightly wounded. While Kilby does not mention Jones's part in the Gardner incident, he does state rather exactly how the chief gunner was silenced: "Before anyone could put him to death, he was wounded in the head and fell, but was not killed."

"I have not yet begun to fight."—Dale in Sherburne 127; JR 146; NWR 297; PR 95; Fanning 42; Cooper 79; Mackenzie 191; Seitz 55, 88; Lorenz 304–5. It is not surprising, recalling the chaotic circumstances at the time, that there is much discrepancy in these early sources over what, exactly, was said by Jones. Still, the accepted version, that given by Dale, so precisely fits the situation and Jones's character, especially when under stress, that there can be little doubt that Jones actually did say "I have not yet begun to fight," or something very close to it. Jones himself in his first report, assuming a formal posture, says simply that he answered "in the most determined negative." It is possible that he actually did not remember his precise words, since he later gave them as "I do not dream of surrendering, but I am determined to make you strike." (NWR 297.) In this phrasing, it is clear, he was attempting to recapture the spirit of something said spontaneously, in the heat of battle, and he has probably been influenced by other versions that had begun to circulate. Somewhat closer to what Dale remembered are the words Jones mentioned to Benjamin Rush about 1782: "No sir, I will not. We have had but a small fight as yet." (*Memorial of Dr. Benjamin Rush,* L. A. Biddle, 1905, p. 121, as quoted in Morison 241). In those days, unfortunately, there were no battle correspondents to give immediate fame to the defiant cries of beleaguered commanders.

A second problem connected with Jones's reply concerns the point in the battle at which the words were said. Morison, strangely enough, concludes that the famous phrase was uttered not near the close of the battle, but at its beginning, during the first collision between the ships. "This is the obvious place for it," Morison remarks in accepting a doubtful statement by Lt. Dale, "not at the end of the battle, which makes no sense." But Dale has certainly stumbled in his recollection of this point (all other primary sources contradict him), and Morison's reasoning on the matter can as easily be made to support a later time instead of an earlier. In reality, it is the earlier time that makes no sense. To announce "I have not yet begun to fight" at the start of a battle transforms the words into nothing but a literal statement of fact, and such a circumstance could hardly have earned immortality for any reply. Only if thundered out in dramatic defiance of a hopeless situation could those fiery words have meant so much and been so well remembered. Further, it is clear, indisputable, that Jones's reply came as the culmination of a series of three events: the release of the prisoners, Gardner's frantic request for quarter, and Pearson's inquiry; and these occurred after 10 P.M., when the battle had been in progress some three hours. This fact was recognized by Morison, but to accommodate it with Dale's statement he has Jones replying twice.

Dale setting the prisoners at the pumps and putting guards at the powder magazine: *Port Folio* 508; NWR 297; Cooper 76; Kilby 32. There is some question as to whether it was Jones who first ordered the prisoners to be herded to the pumps. My reading of the circumstances indicates that Dale probably took the action on his own initiative, though Jones may have given such an order separately.

Mease's return to his post: Note by Jones appended to Mease's deposition in Sherburne 176. According to Jones, the next day Mease's skull was trepanned "in six or seven places," indicating he had probably been hit by grapeshot. Jones also says that Mease behaved in the battle "with distinguished coolness and intrepidity."

Pearson's sole reference to his reasons for surrendering are in his report to the Admiralty: "I found it in vain, and in short impracticable, from the situation we were in, to stand out any longer with the least prospect of success." The assertions by such writers as Mahan, Lorenz and Morison that Pearson struck his colors simply because he had "lost his nerve" (Morison 237) is on its face both unfair and incorrect. Much more went into his decision to strike, as I have tried to show in the narrative, than loss of resolution. Another circumstance which probably played its part, though left unspecified by Pearson, and in fact mentioned by no one at the time or since, was the eighteenth century's prevalent belief that a fight to the finish was nothing but insanity. In those days it was felt that whenever one party gained a clear advantage, an overpowering superiority, then surrender was the only proper course, avoiding unnecessary death, destruction and suffering. To do otherwise, to continue fighting when there was clearly no hope remaining, was looked on almost as barbarity. In this respect Jones may be considered as one of those who helped usher in modern ideas of all-out warfare.

The English prisoner who informed Pearson of the *Richard*'s condition: Sherburne 128; Cooper 78. His last name was preserved in Mease's deposition in Sherburne 175.

The English last-ditch attempt to board the *Richard:* PR 95; TPC 3–4.

"If you have struck . . ."—Middlebrook 46.

Dale's boarding of the *Serapis* and the wounding of Mayrant: Sherburne 128; *Port Folio* 510; Cooper, *Lives,* 79.

The verbal exchange among Dale, Pearson and Wright is recorded by Dale himself in Sherburne 128–9.

"Sir, you have fought . . ."—Fanning 44.

"Well then, it has been diamond . . ."—Fanning 44; Kilby 33. Kilby was stationed on the quarterdeck when the two captains met, and claimed to have been standing within six feet of them. Fanning, too, claims to have been nearby at the time. That the two seamen should have remembered these words, and in nearly the same form (Kilby has it as "It was diamond cut diamond"), is not surprising, since Pearson's remark must have struck his American hearers as an unusual compliment from a defeated English captain, and it was succinctly put. Obliquely, of course, the remark also expressed Pearson's relief that he had not lost his ship to Frenchmen or Spaniards, neither of which was then highly regarded as seamen by the Royal Navy. Eventually Pearson must have learned about the heroic part taken by the French marines, as well as the untrained but staunch Portuguese, not then considered quite diamonds by the English either.

Two further statements by Fanning (44, 45), regarding the meeting of the two captains, have the ring of falsity about them, and have never managed to convince many. When Pearson offered his sword, says Fanning, he did so with the following speech: "It is with the greatest reluctance that I am obliged to resign to you, for it is painful to me, more particularly at this time, when compelled to deliver up my sword to a man who may be said to fight with a halter around his neck!" If this sentiment was uttered at all, I suspect it may have escaped Pearson's lips only later, at the Texel, where he did complain about Jones keeping him in confinement, not allowing him to see the English ambassador. Fanning also says that after their meeting, "The two captains now withdrew into the cabin, and there drank a glass or two of wine together." Morison (239) accepts this outré touch, commenting, "Such were the ceremonial manners of eighteenth century warfare." Perhaps at times, but surely not while nearly three hundred men lay wounded, dying and dead, the decks of both ships slippery with blood, fires raging, and the quarterdeck of the *Richard* about to fall in on top of Jones's cabin. A day or two later aboard the *Serapis,* it may be, Jones and Pearson did share a bottle.

The fall of the *Serapis*'s mainmast: There is

some disagreement over just when the English main-mast went by the board. Pearson himself claimed that it fell at the time he was calling for quarter (PR 96). Morison (237–8) disputes this, saying that the mainmast, though trembling, was upright at the surrender. And that view appears to be the true one. Cooper (79, 81) says that Dale swung aboard the *Serapis* by means of a line hanging from the mainmast's lower yardarm and that the mast stood for another fifteen minutes or so. Kilby (32) re-called that the mast was still standing five minutes after the Englishman struck. Fanning (45) also places the fall sometime after the surrender. Jones gave two views. In his report of 3 October he says that it fell "soon after the captain had come on board." But in NWR 298 he says it went over as Pearson called for quarter. The weight of the evidence seems to be in favor of a later fall, with perhaps a sudden lurch occurring at the moment of surrender.

Part Three
The End of the Bonhomme Richard

The fears of the Americans regarding pursuit by the Royal Navy were well founded. The day after Jones disappeared into the mists of the North Sea, a squadron of eight British warships arrived at Flamborough Head. And within a day or two after that, at least ten more warships had joined in the search (Seitz 56–7; Lorenz 313; Morison 245).

Dale's belated discovery of his wound: *Port Folio* 510; Sherburne 129. The difficulty with the *Serapis*'s anchor is mentioned in the same place in Sherburne.

Jettisoning of the *Richard*'s 18-pounders: Middlebrook 47.

That the *Richard* went down full-rigged is a fact that has so far been overlooked. It is stated clearly by Kilby (33) who mentions "studding sails, topgallant sails, royals, sky-scrapers, and every sail that could be put on a ship—jack, pennants and that beautiful ensign that she so gallantly wore while in action [the flag had been replaced] and when we conquered." Kilby finishes: "Alas she is gone! Never more to be seen!" But, incredible as it may sound, the *Bonhomme Richard* may yet be seen again by mortal eyes. A special American expedition, assisted by the Naval departments of England and France, in 1976 began an effort to find and raise the hulk of the old warship. It has since been announced that the *Richard,* or what remains of her, may actually have been located by sonar.

"But good God . . ."—Fanning 49.

"I shaped my course . . ."—Fanning 51–2; I have slightly condensed Fanning's wordiness in this passage.

"A most glorious sight . . ."—Kilby 33.

"Inexpressible grief . . ."—JR 148.

Part Four
Reckoning

The documents containing the "Charges and Proofs" against Captain Landais were never presented in a court and were eventually deposited in U.S. government files. In 1787 they were published in pamphlet form in New York, in response to Landais's own lame attempt, three years earlier, to explain away all of his questionable actions while in America's service. (*Memorial to Justify the Conduct of Peter Landais' During the Late War*, Boston, 1784.) Sherburne, in 1825, published the "Charges and Proofs," complete, in his documentary biography of Jones. They have not since been reprinted, but copies of Sherburne (also an 1851 revision) are in most large libraries.

For a fuller account of Landais's subsequent fate, see "The Revolution's Caine Mutiny," by Richard B. Morris, *American Heritage*, April 1960. Also, Morison 293–301. That Landais was in command of the *Alliance* during her return to America resulted from another of his mad actions. Removed from the *Alliance* by order of Benjamin Franklin, he actually commandeered the ship while Jones was absent. Jones soon returned, but rather than inflict harm on one of his own vessels, he allowed Landais to sail.

"Was not due primarily . . ."—Mahan 212.

"Cannot have been accidental . . ."—Morison 235.

"Told Captain Landais at . . ."—Sherburne 164.

"They must run away . . ."—Sherburne 165.

"There is in this man . . ."—Adams's diary in Morison 190.

"Not only acquited themselves . . ."—TPC 1–2.

Captain Pearson's honors: *Naval Chronicle,* XXIV, 353, 1810, 360–1. There is no evidence that Jones ever resented the praise and attention heaped on his defeated foe. In fact he managed to make light of the situation, producing a remark that may stand as an example of the wit so often credited to him. At a banquet in France some time in 1780 he was told of Pearson's latest honor, a knighthood, and was asked what he thought of the loser being thus honored. "If I should have the good fortune to fall in with him again," Jones replied, "I shall make him a Lord."

"The largest of the two . . ."—PR 95.

The later adverse reactions to Pearson's explanations about his surrender can be seen in the remark of a writer in *Naval Atlantis* (London, 1789, p. 30), who conjectured that the American would have struck his colors, "had those of the *Serapis* been kept flying two minutes longer." This change in opinion, however, seems not to have hurt Pearson's later career. Within six months he was at sea again, commanding frigate *Alarm,* and later he commanded the *Arethusa.* In 1790 he was assigned a shore post, being made Governor of the Naval Hospital at Greenwich. He died in 1805.

"The share taken by . . ."—Mahan 213.

The rumors about Lt. Stanhope and the testimony at the court-martial: TPC 8–16. The exoneration of Stanhope by the court-martial apparently never reached the ears of the Americans, who, while at the Texel, had become aware of the first rumors. In composing his narrative some twenty years later, Fanning preserved a part of the derogatory tales that had been circulating, casually giving a version of the story as a "singular" circumstance of the battle.

"The extraordinary intrepidity . . ."—NWR 298.

"So brilliant as to excite . . ."—Morison 262.

George Washington's remark occurs in a letter to Jones, Sherburne 235.

"It being night . . ."—Lunt in Sherburne 170. Jones's uncertainty about the whole incident involving Lunt and Ricot may be seen in the following: In his first report, that of 3 October, Jones wrote that Ricot had deliberately kept Lunt out of the battle, "withheld by force the pilot boat with my lieutenant and 15 men." (JR 149–50.) When this statement appeared in the *Leyden Gazette,* which published a portion of the report in late October 1779, Jones wrote the *Gazette:* "Concerning the conduct of Capt. Ricot, I am obliged in honor to declare that, since the action, he has cleared up his conduct in that affair entirely to my satisfaction. It now plainly appears that the lieutenant who was in the pilot-boat, disobeyed the express orders of Capt. Ricot, in not coming to my assistance." (The *Gazette* published the letter and it is quoted in Seitz 136.) The source for the first statement could only have been Lunt, for the second only Ricot, and the discrepancy indicates that more transpired between the two, and between them and Jones, than has reached the existing record. Sometime later, for instance, Jones reverted to the subject in a letter to Lafayette, in which it becomes clear that he is still not quite comfortable with the part played by Ricot: "I beg Captain Ricot's pardon for having said in the extract of my journal that in the engagement with the *Serapis* he prevented my officers and men in the pilot boat from coming to my assistance. I now feel that this did not happen till the pilot boat had returned to the *Vengeance* about the middle of the action, without having boarded the Bonhomme Richard according to Captain Ricot's orders." (Sherburne 156.) I feel that my conclusion in the narrative is the probable one, and that in his vacillation Jones was merely avoiding the necessity of condemning a French officer. Still, Jones's rather cool remark that Lunt and his men had been "mere spectators of the action" (NWR 317) shows that he did have his doubts. It should be noted that Lunt later received a full officer's share of the prize money realized from the entire cruise (Morison 267).

"At least involved a great . . ."—Mackenzie 209.

Captain Cottineau's defection from the Line of Battle: NWR 296; Cooper, *Lives,* 65; Lorenz 291.

Escape of the English sailors from the *Richard* after the battle: NWR 298; Seitz 54; Mackenzie 195. The escapees made shore at Filey, where they gave affidavits before Justice of the Peace Humphrey Osbaldiston, and later before the mayor of Hull. One of these men, Thomas Berry (who said he had been a prisoner of the French for eighteen months and had joined Jones "in hopes of getting his liberty"), inadvertently strengthened Pearson's later false claim that he had surrendered to two ships. Near the end of the fight, deposed Berry, Jones "called to the *Alliance* for assistance, which came up and gave the 40-gun ship [the *Serapis*] a broadside, which being totally disabled, struck." Berry, of course, was in some peril with the British authorities for having served aboard the American ship, and would have avoided saying anything appearing to discredit the *Serapis.*

"The mangled carcasses of . . ."—Fanning 48.

Pearson's inflated estimated of 306 dead and wounded on the *Richard* is in his report, PR 96. The figure was at first widely believed in England and occasioned some argument in the newspapers. As Kilby later sensibly wrote: "If he had killed and wounded that number of us, ought he not to have taken us?" It would be interesting to know just what led Pearson to set down that high figure, more than twice the actual number. The ships had been anchored at the Texel for three days when he dictated his report, but of course confusion still reigned, especially over care of the wounded of both sides. There was also the enormously difficult problem of caring for and feeding the healthy English prisoners, their total now swollen to nearly three hundred. The information could not have come from Jones, for his own early estimate was about 150 dead and wounded. It may have come from the English surgeons who, along with their American counterparts, moved freely among all the wounded, from ship to ship, offering care impartially to Englishman and American alike.

Appendix C

Bibliography

hile the biographical literature on John Paul Jones is extensive, material that deals seriously with the battle against the *Serapis* is comparatively limited. I list here only those sources that have been of some help, direct or indirect, in my research. Fuller listings may be had in Seitz and Lorenz (see below).

Manuscripts

"A court martial held on board His Majesty's Ship Daphne in Sheerness Harbour on Friday the 10th Day of March 1780." Official transcript of the court-martial of Captains Pearson and Piercy, held to investigate the loss of their ships; 17 page original, in PRO Admiralty 1-5315.

"Muster Roll of His Majesty's Ship the Serapis between 1st

September and 7 October 1779." Original in PRO Admiralty 36-7909. Also contains lists and notations on the dead and wounded.

Miscellaneous Correspondence between Captain Richard Pearson and the Admiralty. PRO Admiralty 1-2305. Includes Pearson's report on the battle written 6 October 1779.

Primary

Anon., *"Biographical Memoir of Commodore Dale,"* **The Port Folio,** June 1814, 499–515. (Based on interviews with Dale.)

Barnes, J. S. (ed.), **The Logs of the Serapis—Alliance—Ariel Under the Command of John Paul Jones, 1779–1780,** Naval History Society, New York 1911. (From the original volume now in the New York Historical Society.)

"Charges and Proofs Respecting the Conduct of Peter Landais." In Sherburne (see below) 162–177. Consists of itemized charges with individual attestation by nineteen officers of the squadron. Also, eleven first-person depositions, including those of Lts. Lunt and Stack, Midshipmen Fanning, Coram, Mayrant and Linthwaite, and purser Matthew Mease. First published in pamphlet form, New York, 1787; originals in **Papers of the Continental Congress,** National Archives.

Dale, Lt. Richard, *"Particulars of the Engagement Between the Bonhomme Richard and the Serapis,"* in Sherburne (see below) 126–129.

Fanning, Nathaniel, **Memoirs of NF, an Officer of the American Navy, 1778–1783, The Magazine of History,** Extra No. 21, New York 1913. First published privately, New

York 1806. In later printings it is designated as *"Narrative of NF,"* and by that name it is now generally known.

Jones, John Paul, Report to Benjamin Franklin, dated 3 October 1779, in **John Paul Jones Commemoration at Annapolis, April 24, 1906,** Washington, Government Printing Office, 1907 (reprinted 1966). This long letter-report (some 6500 words, of which about one-third concerns the battle) has been many times reprinted, though usually only in part. This volume contains the entire text.

Jones, John Paul, *"Paul Jones"* (title supplied by the magazine), **Niles's Weekly Register,** June–July 1812. A brief autobiography originally written in English by Jones and translated into French by Benoit Andrè for presentation to Louis XVI in 1786. The English original is lost; this is a retranslation from the French.

Kilby, John, *"Narrative of John Kilby,"* **Scribner's Magazine,** V. 38, 1905, 23–41.

Landais, Pierre, **Memorial to Justify the Conduct of Peter Landais During the Late War,** Peter Edes, Boston, 1784.

Middlebrook, T. (ed.), **The Log of the Bonhomme Richard,** Mystic, Conn., 1936. The entry concerning the day of the battle is very brief, setting forth the bare facts in usual laconic logbook style, with some usual logbook errors. There are few details of the battle itself. A second, longer log entry concerning the engagement was written into the log of the *Serapis* by Lt. Hunt, probably at the dictation of Jones, and is herein reprinted. Also contains a portion of Fanning's **Narrative,** and the *Richard*'s muster roll (from the original in the New York Historical Society, where it is laid into the original log of the *Serapis*).

Pearson, Capt. Richard, Report to the Admiralty, dated 6 October 1779. In Seitz (see below) 93–98, also in Sherburne (see below) 129–132. So far as appears, Pearson wrote only this one brief, official account of the battle, and left no other comments on record anywhere. His present traceable descendents possess none of his papers.

Seitz, Don, **JPJ, His Exploits in English Seas During 1778– 1780,** New York, 1917. Collects contemporary newspaper reports and accounts of the battle and related matters.

A note on the "Filkin Manuscripts"—A gift to the British Museum in 1864, these four notebooks collect contemporary newspaper, magazine and book excerpts on John Paul Jones' activities in Europe, along with miscellaneous documents. They were first used by Lorenz for his biography of Jones, but Morison (432) rejects them as "worthless," while giving no reason for that judgment. I have not used them, preferring to work with the original documents, but in view of Morison's unexplained condemnation some word about them may be of value.

According to the copy made for the New York Historical Society, they are the work of one Richard Filkin, M.D., of Richmond, Surrey, who explains his interest by saying that his father was a Midshipman on the *Serapis,* and fought in the battle. There was indeed a Richard Filkin aboard the *Serapis* (Muster roll, Admiralty 36-7909). He was not, however, a Midshipman. He entered in May 1779 as Able Seaman, later being promoted to Master's Mate. The probability is that he was still aboard four months later and did take part in the battle.

Those entries in the Filkin notebooks that I have been able to check prove to be faithful copies of the originals—the court martial of Captain Pearson, for instance, and Pearson's letters to the Admiralty. A legitimate conclusion would be that these painfully compiled, if random, excerpts are in fact quite trustworthy—true at least, that is, to their sources. Unfortunately, with regard to the battle, they contain nothing of importance that is not also available in the originals.

Secondary

Allen, Gardner, **Naval History of the American Revolution,** Boston, 1913.

Chapelle, H. L., **History of the American Sailing Navy,** New York, 1949.

Clowes, W. L., **The Royal Navy,** London, 1897.

Coggins, Jack, **Ships and Seamen of the American Revolution,** Promontory Press, 1969.

Cooper, James F., **History of the United States Navy,** Philadelphia, 1839.

Cooper, James F., **The Lives of Distinguished American Naval Officers,** Philadelphia, 1846. Contains chapters on Jones and Dale, giving information obtained in personal interviews with Dale himself.

Edinburgh Memoirs (no author or editor listed). Published in the U.S. as **Life of Rear-Admiral JPJ,** Philadelphia, 1845. Reprint of a volume originally issued in 1830 in Edinburgh under the supervision of Jones's neice, Mrs. Janette Taylor.

Gurn, Joseph, **Commodore John Barry,** New York, 1933. Contains scattered references to both Jones and Dale, as well as information on the Continental Navy.

Laughton, J., *"Paul Jones, Pirate,"* **Fraser's Magazine,** London, April 1878, 501–522.

Lorenz, Lincoln, **JPJ, Fighter for Freedom and Glory,** U.S. Naval Institute, 1943.

Mackenzie, A. S., **Life of JPJ,** Boston, 1841.

Mahan, A. T., *"JPJ in the Revolution,"* **Scribner's Magazine,** v. 29, 1898, 204–219.

Mahan, A. T., **Major Operations of Navies in the American War of Independence,** Boston, 1913.

Morison, S. E., **JPJ, A Sailor's Biography,** Boston, 1959.

Morris, R. B., *"The Revolution's Caine Mutiny,"* **American Heritage,** April 1960 (Concerning Landais).

Nicodème, *"Notice Historique sur le Bonhomme Richard,"* **Revue Maritime,** v. 173, 1907, 545–554.

Sands, R., **Life and Correspondence of JPJ,** New York, 1830.

Sherburne, J. H., **Life and Character of the Chevalier JPJ,** Washington, 1825.

Warner, O., *"The Action off Flamborough Head,"* **American Heritage,** August 1963.

Acknowledgments

For timely and generous aid of various sorts I wish to return my thanks to the following: Mr. Timothy Walsh, Mr. Bruce Lee, Mr. Reginald Braggonier, Mr. Walter Hunt, Miss Merial Larkin, Miss Janetta Macpherson, Mrs. Carol Tarlow, Mr. Edgar Hinchcliffe, Mr. Alan Brocklebank, Rev. Kenneth Cove, Miss Gay Oughton, the staff of the New York Public Library Reading Room at 42nd Street, New York, the County Councils of Lancashire and Cumbria.

For their forebearance, an essential aid to any writer, I offer humble thanks to my family.

Index

Battle (*cont.*)
English prisoners released, 79–80, 82, 84, 157
Jones's death, rumor of, 79
boarding:
attempts, 57–58, 64–65, 67, 74–75, 77–78, 147, 148–149, 150
English, 85–86, 150
Jones resolves on, 41–42, 146–147
clearing out enemy sharpshooters, 42, 58, 65, 67, 147, 151
bursting of old guns on *Richard*, 39–40, 99
loss of eighteen-pounders, 40, 135, 146
casualties, 115–117, 167–168
English officers meet Jones, 88–89
fires, 67, 72–73, 81, 85, 153
firing commenced, 38–39
firing at English mainmast, 60, 150
mast cracked, 86
mast down, 89, 160–161
grenade destroys English guns, 68–71, 151–153
Jones refuses to strike, 64, 78, 82, 85, 155–157
leaks, repairing; pumping, 39, 63, 78, 82, 84, 157
ship sinking, 79, 85
maneuvering at close quarters, 43–47, 52, 147–149
heavy English firing, 46
one of the bloodiest between two sailing ships, 115–117

Pallas and *Countess of Edinburgh*, 52–54
Pearson's dilemma, 71–72, 83–84, 108–109
Pearson strikes, 86–87, 88
ships indistinguishable in smoke and darkness, 53, 55, 104–105
ships linked and lashed, 47–49
English blow off gun ports, 51
English guns tear *Richard*, 58–59, 67, 73–74, 85
furious hour's fighting, 56–57
locked bow to stern, 50
Serapis anchors, 49
side to side, 49–50
superiority of *Serapis*, 41, 59
Vengeance refuses to fight, 55
Beilby, Samuel, 149
Berry, Thomas, 167
Bonhomme Richard (frigate), xii, 10–12, 37, 101, 103, 104, 105, 118
armament, 19, 31, 140
casualties in the battle, 116–117, 167–168
dead, 129–130
wounded, 131–132
crew, 19–21, 22–23, 140, 141–142
officers, 21–22
end of:
afire after battle, 91, 94, 95
burial of dead, 96
cut loose from *Serapis*, 92
danger from Royal Navy, 91–92, 161–162